INFORMATION

This book provides a comprehensive, easy-to-understand introductory guide to information, offering students the critical tools they need to shift their positioning from consumers and users to creators and critics.

Searching, accessing, and using information are central to most daily lives. Yet, many users are not able to define what information is, identify who controls information, and create information to achieve a common good. In this book, Micky Lee teaches readers to critically interrogate key issues such as the categorization of information and knowledge throughout history, what digital divides are, why information is gender- and race-biased, how governments and corporations control citizens and consumers, as well as how we can resist unbalanced power relations. Readers will not only be able to relate these issues to "old" technologies, such as writing and printing, but will also be able to examine futurist technologies through the lenses of these enduring issues.

A thoughtful and comprehensive overview, this is an ideal book for students and scholars of media studies, information and society, and communication and technology.

Micky Lee is Professor of Media Studies at Suffolk University, Boston, MA, USA. She has published in the areas of feminist political economy, information, technologies, and finance. Her latest books are *Media technologies for work and play in East Asia: Critical perspectives on Japan and the two Koreas, Alphabet, Understanding the business of global media in the digital age*, and *Bubbles and machines: Gender, information, and financial crises*.

KEY IDEAS IN MEDIA AND CULTURAL STUDIES

The *Key Ideas in Media and Cultural Studies* series covers the main concepts, issues, debates and controversies in contemporary media and cultural studies. Titles in the series constitute authoritative, original essays rather than literary surveys, but are also written explicitly to support undergraduate teaching. The series provides students and teachers with lively and original treatments of key topics in the field.

Reality TV
Annette Hill

Culture
Ben Highmore

Representation
Jenny Kidd

Celebrity
Sean Redmond

Global Cultural Economy
Christiaan De Beukelaer and Kim-Marie Spence

Marxism
Karl Marx's Fifteen Key Concepts for Cultural
and Communication Studies
Christian Fuchs

Deep Mediatization
Andreas Hepp

Information
Micky Lee

For more information about this series, please visit: https://www.routledge.com/Key-Ideas-in-Media—Cultural-Studies/book-series/KEYIDEA

INFORMATION

Micky Lee

NEW YORK AND LONDON

First published 2021
by Routledge
605 Third Avenue, New York, NY 10158

and by Routledge
2 Park Square, Milton Park, Abingdon, Oxon, OX14 4RN

Routledge is an imprint of the Taylor & Francis Group, an informa business

© 2021 Taylor & Francis

The right of Micky Lee to be identified as author of this work has been asserted by her in accordance with sections 77 and 78 of the Copyright, Designs and Patents Act 1988.

All rights reserved. No part of this book may be reprinted or reproduced or utilised in any form or by any electronic, mechanical, or other means, now known or hereafter invented, including photocopying and recording, or in any information storage or retrieval system, without permission in writing from the publishers.

Trademark notice: Product or corporate names may be trademarks or registered trademarks, and are used only for identification and explanation without intent to infringe.

Library of Congress Cataloging-in-Publication Data
A catalog record for this book has been requested

ISBN: 978-0-367-89776-5 (hbk)
ISBN: 978-0-367-85872-8 (pbk)
ISBN: 978-1-003-02105-6 (ebk)

Typeset in Times New Roman
by Apex CoVantage, LLC

Contents

1	Introduction: What Do We Do with Information?	1
2	Defining	27
3	Searching	57
4	Accessing	80
5	Using	111
6	Creating	142
7	Conclusion: Can We Do More with Information?	171
	Index	186

1

INTRODUCTION
WHAT DO WE DO WITH INFORMATION?

INTRODUCTION

We search for, use, and create an abundant amount of diverse information every day. Our interactions with information shape who we are, our relationships with each other, and the society in which we live. Since information plays such a prominent role in our lives, we need to examine what it is, what we do with it, and what it does to us. To unpack these big questions, we will use a daily life example to show why they matter.

Let us sit in a subway train and observe what commuters do with information. Even within a short subway ride, we interact with an abundant amount of information. Some read a physical book, others surf the web on their smartphones, yet others get a head start with work on the laptop. Some stare at the ads inside the subway, others may simply observe their fellow commuters. The commuters are so engrossed in the information of their choice that they rarely pay attention to the conductor's announcements and almost never engage fellow commuters in conversations. Out of the commuters' earshot, information exchanges take place to ensure a smooth subway ride: train conductors communicating with each other and computer-automated traffic signals instructing the drivers to go or stop. In addition, there is some information that the commuters already know by heart, such as the subway map and train frequency.

The information with which we interact is as diverse as it is abundant: some is analogue (such as words on a page), some digital (such as words on a webpage) (Floridi, 2010); some is constantly updated (such as stock prices), others not (such as subway map); some is initiated by the users (such as surfing the web), some initiated by technologies (such as traffic signals).

Despite our constant interactions with information, we rarely stop and think too much about information until the systems break down. For example, during a power outage, we cannot access the Internet at home so we resort to analogue information, such as books and board games. In another example, after the two bombs exploded in Boston Marathon in 2013, there was such a frenzy of online communication that it was impossible for onlookers to call their loved ones or check the Internet for news.

When information systems work again, most may feel a sense of relief, but may also lament how much we depend on online information. Many feel burdened by information overload and seek to manage their interactions with information. Ironically, some solutions are phone apps that promise to select and organize information better! In addition, we worry that the amount of screen time will make us lose human connections with others, so we use apps to count screen time and to remind us to go offline. If information does bring convenience to modern lives but also creates problems, then we need to dream up a better way to interact with information so that it enriches our lives without controlling them.

To dream of a better way to interact with information, we need to question *who* made the decisions about information, *how* and *why* they did it. We need to understand how these decisions made our interactions with information appear to be natural and inevitable. More importantly, we need to understand *who* decides the way that we interact with information and *why* they have the power to do so. These are big questions and we will return to the commuter example again.

Subway trains run on a time schedule. Passengers know that scheduled trains are necessary for us to plan our commutes to work.

However, we need to ask what kind of society would need a train schedule and how the train schedule constitutes this kind of society. The train schedule is a recent invention in human history—humans had coped for centuries even without any fixed schedule. However, the train schedule became necessary when the train became a major method of transportation. To avoid train collisions, companies had to plan. The implications of time schedules, however, are broader. For one thing, they rely on standardized time, which in turn validates why schedules are necessary (Preda, 2009). If time had not been standardized, then trains would have still collided with each other even if they run on schedule. Standardized time means time is no longer fluid and subjective, locals would rely less on the sundial but more on the church clock that is set to standardized time. When time became something objective, it could then be counted, estimated, and rationalized (Grossberg, 1996). Therefore, we could count the hours left at work, we could estimate how much time it takes to commute, and we could decide whether some tasks are worth the time. While these all sound natural and inevitable, *who* benefits when time is made objective?

Standardized time and more precise time-keeping devices are imperative to industrialization (O'Carroll, 2008; Winchester, 2018). In pre-industrial time, humans worked on farms on a more fluid schedule. While farmers had to observe the hours of the day and the seasons of the year for their farming activities, they did not have to count the hours that they work. However, when they moved to cities and worked in factories, counting work hours became imperative because their wages were calculated based on the duration of time for which they worked. Accounting for time benefits factory owners more than workers because they could calculate more accurately how many labor hours to buy. In contrast, workers could not stop working even if they produced more than enough. Nowadays, few in developed economies may work in factories, but many have dead-end jobs that pay an hourly wage with few benefits and little prospects. Similar to factory workers, workers in these dead-end jobs are expected to arrive at the workplace on time and not leave early. To these workers, trains that run on time are extremely important because constant lateness could make them lose their jobs. Is there another way to see information so that how much one makes is not calculated based on time?

If we are going to imagine a society in which we interact with information differently, we ought to design another system that ensures work is meaningful. For example, a lot of childcare workers are paid by the hour, but what parents seek is not the *time* that they are on the job, but the *care* that they provide. If this is the case, their wage should be determined by the positive social value that they create, not merely the time that they spend on the job. In other words, what matters to parents is the quality of social goods provided by the childcare workers, not just the number of hours that they work.

To imagine a better society would require us to assume a different position to interact with information. We cannot approach information from those of end users and consumers, instead we need to see ourselves as information critics and activists. Moving from a passive to an active position would help us understand how power relates to information by asking *who* can decide for whom *how* to interact with information. In addition, as critics and activists, we ask *why*: Why is power structured in such a way that some can make the decision while most of us cannot? If we are able to assume an active position from where we ask who, how, and why, we will find out why our interactions with information appear to be natural even though it is not. In the following, I argue that a critical perspective will aid us in this transformative process.

A CRITICAL PERSPECTIVE TO INFORMATION: WHAT IT IS AND WHAT IT DOES

In order to explain why information is centralized yet taken for granted in our daily lives, we will use a critical perspective to examine information in this book. This perspective highlights the underlying political, economic, cultural, and social contexts under which information is produced, distributed, and consumed. Production refers to the process of creating information; distribution refers to the dissemination of information from the producers to the consumers; consumption refers to the final stage when users interact with the information for different purposes.

A critical perspective argues that information is not external to politics, economy, culture, and society. Information does not precede any society, it is not a "thing" that exists before humans organize themselves politically, economically, and culturally. In fact, humans need information to form political communities, conduct economic exchanges, and create cultural goods. Therefore, we argue that information *constitutes* society. How and what information is produced, distributed, and consumed forms specific kinds of society. In some societies, only a small number of people can produce and distribute information, these societies are usually called closed societies. In other societies, many people can produce and distribute information, they are called free and open societies. While an open society is seen to be better than a closed one because it allows for a freer exchange of information, we must reject the view that an information-rich society is naturally better than an information-poor one. What it means is that a society with many information producers is not *naturally* more advanced, progressive and democratic than one with few producers. The quantity of information produced and exchanged should not determine how good or bad a society is because we also have to question what kinds of information are out there.

Information is not politically, economically, and culturally neutral (Segev, 2010). What it means is that someone somewhere at some points decide what kinds of information to produce, how to circulate it, and who will consume it. These decisions are always motivated by political, economic, or cultural reasons. Advertisers, marketers, celebrities, journalists, politicians are social actors who are able to sway public opinion, but most of us—through daily activities such as posting on social media, chatting with friends—can also influence the opinions of a few people. We may ask our friends to change their consumption habits or persuade them to take political action.

Another reason to explain why information is not neutral is because information is always embedded in technologies through which it is produced, distributed, and consumed. Information can *not* exist on its own without technologies. Some technologies are low-tech (such as paper and pen), others high-tech (such as an algorithm that processes a large quantity of information). The technologies that enable the production, distribution, and consumption of information also gives meanings to information. For example, some high-end boutiques ask sale associates to hand-write thank-you notes for customers. The use of paper and pen is supposed to show customers that the sale associates genuinely care about them as people. As a result, we are likely to remember a hand-written thank-you note than an email. Because the meanings of information are embedded in technologies, information does not have a universal and monolithic characteristic, the technologies that produce it always constitute how it is understood and used in specific contexts (Babe, 1995).

A Boston Example

To illustrate how information constitutes society and why information is not neutral, let us consider what information may mean to a Boston resident who lived 200 years ago. If we compare lives then and now without using a critical perspective, some may simply conclude that lives then were worse because there was not much information. If we use a critical perspective, then we will need to understand how information constituted a society two centuries ago.

A Bostonian who lived in 1820 had little information to seek and process, and the variety of information was limited as well. Some might have got news and gossips from family members and acquaintances, others might have relied on publications to learn about the outside world. Some contemporary Bostonians may envy this kind of life because the earlier residents probably did not suffer from information overload and constant digital interruptions. They may also envy the earlier residents for their more meaningful and long-lasting personal relationships because they sought information from one another.

However, when we consider *who* were more likely to produce, circulate, and consume information, we will notice that only certain people were allowed to do so. Those who could do so probably already had some power in society because of their professions or wealth. The limited information sources was a problem because it was difficult to verify how accurate information was. This meant that the information source was of great importance: if the source was deemed credible, then the information would be deemed accurate. In turn, credibility of the information source would have been seen as identical as social power. Therefore, educated male elites who had more social power would have been seen as the only legitimate information sources in Boston. Women, servants, former slaves, and uneducated populations were excluded from information production because they were not believed to be credible sources.

The question then is: How does an unbalanced access to information production constitute unbalanced power relations in society? How are both kinds of power imbalance mutually reinforced so that they were maintained? Two centuries ago, education was reserved for a small number of people; there was no formal education institutions for women, non-whites, and immigrants. As a result, these populations were not considered to be literate enough to run the government or to conduct businesses. When these populations were banned from participating in public life, they were deemed to have little need for information for they were not in charge of decision-making. The exclusion from education, public life participation, and decision-making all reinforced a belief that certain populations were intellectually inferior; this belief in turn became an explanation why they did not need information access or formal education. The false belief of intellectual inferiority justified why inequalities between gender, race, and class needed to maintain; such inequalities both manifest *and* explain an unequal access to information.

Even though most Bostonians of today would not agree that certain populations are naturally more intellectually inferior and they may not approve blatant inequalities, we have to be cautious to claim that information access is now equal because of more egalitarian social relations. The COVID-19 pandemic demonstrates why information access is still unequal because of unequal social relations. The pandemic has disproportionately affected immigrants and communities of color. At the earliest stage, most of the public information was disseminated in English (Gamboa, 2020) even though Spanish-speaking communities were hit harder by the virus. The abrupt closing of schools also left low-income children—many of them living in immigrant households or communities of color—not having appropriate technologies for online learning (Smith & Reeves, 2020). Even though Boston is an affluent city and the government vows to provide equal opportunities for all, an unplanned event like a pandemic revealed many deep-rooted social inequalities constituted by race and class.

To conclude, the above examples of past and present Boston show that no society—information-rich or information-poor—is inherently good or bad. In different societies at different times, decisions are made to determine what kinds of information is produced, distributed, and consumed. While some consequences are intentional—such as barring certain populations from having an education—others are not—such as not foreseeing difficulties with online learning among low-income children. In addition, different societies have conflicting views of how information should be organized. Some societies believe that there will be fewer conflicts if only a few can control information, others believe that societies can only thrive if as many people can produce information as possible.

While each society should have autonomy to decide how information should be used and produced, the different attitudes towards information in a globalized world could have dire results for most of the world populations. For example, Hollywood has long seen films as private goods, so those who reproduce films without permission are deemed as thieves. There is little regard paid to the fact that some societies do not see reproduced films as illegal. Yet, the disagreement about what information is also opens up possibilities for activists, artists, and critics to shape the future of information. For example, information is critical to achieve some goals, such as common goods, social justice, and equality. In the following, I will give a brief summary of a critical perspective of media studies and suggest what some common goals of critical scholars are.

A VERY SHORT HISTORY OF A CRITICAL PERSPECTIVE OF MEDIA STUDIES

The Very Beginning

Scholars critically examined the relationship between media and society long before digital technologies were invented and popularized. When cinema gained popularity, Frankfurt School intellectuals (such as Horkheimer & Adorno, 2006) examined how popular culture gave joy to the masses who sought relaxation after a grueling day at work. However, they did not see films as artistic work. They believed that films are standardized products that were mass produced for capitalists to make money. Popular culture provided workers with brief moments of joy which prevented them from questioning class oppression. As such, the capitalists who hired the workers and those who made popular media worked hand in hand to protect their economic interests. To the Frankfurt School intellectuals, popular culture was unlikely to free workers from class exploitation, but was an ideological product to quench workers' dissatisfaction to reinforce the unequal social relation between capitalists and workers.

Frankfurt School intellectuals developed their arguments of ideology and class exploitation from Karl Marx's (1999) analysis of class relations between capitalists and workers during the height of the Industrial Revolution in England. Marx asked why capitalists got richer while workers had to keep on working just to get by. He argued that workers, unlike capitalists, only had one commodity to sell, which is their labor time. On a workday, they sold some of their labor time to make money to sustain lives such as buying food and paying rent. But some of the workday was spent to make profits for the owners, and the profits were not shared with the workers. If the workers only had to work to sustain their lives, they would not have had to work for such a long day. However, workers were not in a position to revolt because capitalists owned the means of production (such as the weaving looms), so they could continue reaping the profits from workers who had no choice but to continue selling their labor time to capitalists.

To ensure that this exploitative system kept on functioning, the ruling class also relied on class ideology to justify why such unequal class relation is necessary (Marx & Engels, 2006). The ruling class maintained a false consciousness, a worldview that suggests what society is *naturally* like. False consciousness is not lies or deception, but a belief system. In the past, God's power was used to explain why certain people are kings and others are peasants. Even though few people subscribe to a divine explanation nowadays, but many may still believe that royalty is essential to national pride and national history.

Cultural Studies, Political Economy, Science and Technology Studies

In the late 1970s, critical scholars began to draw on the writings of Marx and the Frankfurt School to understand a mass media society in which popular culture plays a more prominent role in modern life and identity construction. The Centre for Contemporary Cultural Studies at the University of Birmingham became the birthplace of British

Cultural Studies where scholars such as Stuart Hall (1973), Angela McRobbie (1978), and Dick Hebdige (1979) called attention to the importance of mediated popular culture in shaping class identities in a class-based society. They argued that the media legitimize a middle-class ideology, which sees the interest of the ruling class as that of all classes. This ideology marginalizes working-class interests in public discourse such as broadcast news (Morley, 1980). For example, workers' strikes are likely to be portrayed as a disruption to the economy and daily lives rather than as social justice.

On the other side of the Atlantic Ocean, political economic scholars began to notice the growing size of media and telecommunications corporations as well as their close relationships with the government and the military. One landmark book that shed light on the "industrial military complex" is Herbert Schiller's *Who knows: Information in the age of the Fortune 500* (1981) in which he argued that U.S. government corporations heavily invested in communication technologies and telecommunications in the 1970s to combat slow economic growth and inflation. During that time, the U.S. was eager to move manufacturing jobs abroad and to quench developing countries' opposition to American imperialism (Robins, 1982). The development of information and technologies sectors can then be seen as a strategy that the U.S. used to reinforce American imperialism that continues to these days. For example, the most valued information and communication technologies corporations, such as Apple, Microsoft, Alphabet (parent company of Google), and Facebook are all based in the U.S.

The divergent paths of inquiry chosen by British cultural studies scholars and American political economists have paved ways for media studies scholars to critically examine the relationship between information and society as culture, economy, and politics. In this book, I use four approaches under the umbrella of critical perspective to guide the discussion of information and society: (1) political economy; (2) critical cultural studies; (3) feminist theories; and (4) critical race theories. While political economists were the earliest to look at the industries of new information and communication technology and their implications on society, the proliferation of digital media such as video games, platforms, apps, and search engines has blurred the boundary between "mass media" and "communication technologies", which probed critical cultural studies scholars, feminists, and critical race theorists to pay attention to the consumption of information in the everyday lives.

Political economists such as Robert Babe (2010), Christian Fuchs (2016), Dal Yong Jin (2015), Armand Mattelart (2003), Vincent Mosco (2004), Dan Schiller (2007), Janet Wasko (Mosco & Wasko, 1988) have written extensively on a political economy of information since Herbert Schiller (1981, 1989) first offered his insights. They agreed with Schiller that the speedy development of information and communication technologies since the 1970s was a response to slow economic growth in developed countries. Transnational corporations, governments, and the military all fueled the development with private interests in mind. They also pointed out that private interests turned information, a public resource, into a commercial product. Consequently, privatization of information erodes the sense of citizenship because the markets determine the relationship that users have with information. Gradually we ask how much something cost to us rather than how useful information is to society.

At the same time, the pervasiveness of digital information harms workers in at least four ways: first, workers are segregated into high-paying information-intensive jobs and low-paying service jobs (Hardt & Negri, 1993). High-tech workers for transnational companies are what Fuchs (2013) called aristocrats. These workers enjoy many more privileges and job benefits than the invisible workers who serve them, such as cafeteria workers and janitors (Lee, 2019). Second, workers' productivity is monitored by information technologies; call center managers count how many calls are answered and how satisfied the customers are. Third, the wealth created by information and technologies is not evenly distributed. The income gap between those who own the most and those who own the least has been increasing in the U.S. (Horowitz, Igielnik, & Kochhar, 2020). Fourth, a platform economy creates harsh competition among workers. For example, during the COVID-19 pandemic, there was a surge of grocery shoppers, and workers needed to respond to requests quickly while receiving positive feedback from customers, in order to stay in the game (Brandom, 2020). The irony is that they are referred to as independent, self-employed entrepreneurs who enjoy flexibility on the job.

Cultural studies scholars have also written about information technologies extensively when digital technologies blurred the once-presumed distinction between mass media and information. Nowadays, media content such as news stories, television shows, and films are commonly consumed on a mobile phone. Video games, apps, and social media also expand the boundary of information and entertainment media. Cultural studies scholars rarely study information as it is, instead they tend to focus on specific technologies and how audiences interpret them. Some technologies that interested them are: the iPhone (Hjorth, Burgess, & Richardson, 2012), self-monitoring lifestyle apps (Lupton, 2016), YouTube (Burgess & Green, 2018), Twitter (Murthy, 2018), online streaming services (Lobato, 2019), the Internet of Things (Bunz & Meikle, 2018), search engines (Halavais, 2017), car-sharing platforms (John, 2016), and algorithms (Goffey, 2008; Kitchin, 2014; MacKenzie, 2005). Cultural studies scholars do not believe that users passively consume information provided by corporations, instead they engage in interactive exchanges and use an array of tools to interpret information (Curtin, 2009). Users may also create information in ways that are not anticipated by corporations (Jenkins, 2009). While some cultural studies scholars believe in the power of users' agency, others tend to believe that corporations shape and limit users' agency.

While political economists focus on the power of corporations and cultural studies scholars focus on the power of (or lack of) the audience, one question that fascinates both political economists and cultural studies scholars is why consumers produce a large amount of information on social media even though they know that they don't get paid. Political economists believe that users have no choice because if they don't agree that corporations could use their information, then they cannot use the "free" services. Therefore, the price to pay for the free services is to sell information, akin to factory workers selling their labor time (Smythe, 1977). On the other hand, cultural studies scholars believe that an online identity is constructed through information. Concepts such as social capital and affect economy illustrate that users gain credibility and pleasure even if they do not get paid. The concept "social capital" suggests that users gain online reputation by having followers (Utz, 2016); the concept "affect economy" suggests that users' feeling of personal satisfaction in online activities is as important as money transaction. Therefore, cultural studies scholars would believe that users' activities cannot be solely constrained and explained by the markets alone. However, political economists would also ask whether online users, like factory workers, operate under a false consciousness maintained by corporations. In other words, if the advertising and marketing of online activities are said to be fun and enjoyable, whether users are convinced that this is indeed the case.

Both political economists and cultural studies have not adequately examined the agency of technology because they believe that humans are the sole actors to exercise agency in human–technology interaction (see Braman, 2006). Science and Technology Studies scholars (Callon, 1991; Latour, 1993; Law, 1999; Woolgar, 1991) argue that machines (such as the smartphone and the computer) also have a sense of agency; their existence asks users to act on them (Callon & Law, 1995). In the words of Woolgar (1991), technology is understood vis-à-vis the actors and capability of humans and other animate entities. The introduction of new technologies modifies our understanding of the differences between animate and inanimate entities. The belief that machines have an agency marks a break from cultural studies scholarship on "older" technologies (such as television) that are not assumed to have a sense of agency. After all, we believe that viewers choose television channels, the television set does not choose content for us. In contrast, a smartphone can see, hear, and track the users' activities (Bunz & Meikle, 2018). The smartphone produces and processes information that asks humans to react to it. One good example is the buzzes and sounds made by a smartphone that demand users to pick it up and act upon the notifications. In the age of smart machines, there is a reciprocal relationship between objects and subjects, humans and non-human entities (Wajcman & Jones, 2012). In the words of Lievrouw (2014), the material affordances of technologies means "the physical properties or features of objects and settings that invites actors to use them in particular ways" (p. 23).

Feminist and Critical Race Theories

Gender and race provide vantage points from where information can be critiqued. When the Internet gained popularity in the general population, scholars studied the relationship between race and gender by treating them as variables in the use of information. They were interested in understanding how users of different genders and races interact with information. These studies were not viewed through a critical lens. Instead, they reinforced the norm of information use because white males from the developed world are assumed to be the norm against which others are compared. These studies reinforce that there is a correct way to use information, and that way should be followed by users who are not the targets of technology companies. For example, there are many reports on the low number of female students in computing sciences (National Center for Women and Information Technology, 2007; Ramsey & McCorduck, 2005; Simard, 2007), but they do not name who form the majority of computing sciences students and critique how the majority has more power to create norms.

Feminists and critical race theorists instead ask why there is an assumed normative way to use information, who regulate this correct way to use information, and who benefit from maintaining such norms. Some earliest writings of Ursula Huws (2003, 2013), Lisa McLaughlin (2005), Juliet Webster (1995), Gillian Youngs (2005) asked these questions by examining the implications of information and communication technologies on gender relations. They are particularly interested in investigating how technologies shape women's paid and unpaid work. Governments and politicians have hailed information technologies as a liberating tool for women because they are believed to bring employment opportunities to women who have to take care of the household (Sterne & Stabile, 2003). However, feminist scholars cautioned against such optimism. They did not think that technologies have made women's work more flexible, instead they further exploit women's labor because women are asked to do two jobs at once—one unpaid at home, one underpaid at the telecommuting job. In addition to the stress of doing two jobs at once, women's work is made invisible by technologies because this income is supposed to supplement the money that (a presumably male) spouse brings home. Therefore, their paid and unpaid labor is devalued by information technologies. In some cases, technologies have replaced women's labor (Bryceson, 1985). To examine how technologies shape gender relations, Youngs (2005) suggested that feminists should examine the question of access from a historical perspective.

Since the early 2000, there has been a rise of post-feminism, a belief that gender relations have been achieved so there is no need for women and their allies to fight for more rights. Media technologies are seen as tools that women can use to form their female subjectivity (Ormrod, 1995). While technologies have been useful for women—especially those who had been denied a voice in mainstream media—to self-represent themselves to a wider audience, they are also tools for women to self-exploit. In some cases, women are asked to see themselves as entrepreneurs who can set up online businesses on social media (Jang, 2021). In other cases, women re-claim their sexuality by posing "sexy" pictures of themselves on social media. While it is true that these women take charge of the technologies that channel their sexuality, these images invite "male gaze", feeding into male heterosexual desire (Abidin & Thompson, 2012).

Similar to feminists, critical race theorists do not think digital technologies have solved structural problems caused by inequalities. In many ways, such inequalities transcend from the offline world to the online world. In some ways, inequalities are exacerbated in the online world because online participation can be exclusive and the anonymity of racial harassment promotes white supremacy. Jessie Daniels (2012) argued that understanding race online requires a holistic perspective. She wrote that multilayered structural racism underlies the Internet. For example, the labor force in Silicon Valley is racially segregated (Lee, 2019); website design classifies races and ethnicities and enforce their distinctions (Nakamura, 2007); online representations of non-whites are racist, and the bodies of black women are commodified (Noble, 2018); misinformation is easily circulated about race because white supremacists would search for untrue information to confirm their beliefs (Daniels, 2009). The COVID-19 pandemic also brought to surface one fundamental inequality about the online world: that children from communities of color are less likely to have Internet access and computer devices at home when compared to their white counterparts. Even though the smartphone has narrowed the online access gap between races (Perrin & Turner, 2019), the matter of ownership of a personal computer among households of different races still points to the stubborn reality of information inequality.

I have briefly summarized how four critical perspectives—political economy, critical cultural studies, feminist theories, and critical race studies—understand information. Even though it appears that theorists of these four perspectives do not always agree with each other, the messy but constitutive relationship between information and society requires more than one theoretical approach because each of them has both strengths and limitations. The political economic perspective illuminates the structure of the information industries, which benefits capitalists and harms workers but it does not pay enough attention to how users make meanings of information and construct identities as critical cultural studies scholars do. Feminist and critical race theories shed light on how gender and race provide vantage points to critique industry structure, labor exploitation, and identity formation. Both vantage points enrich a political economic and cultural analysis of information. Despite some disagreements between these four perspectives, they are tied together by their attempts to illuminate the role that power plays in the circulation of capital and meanings in and through information.

HOW DOES A CRITICAL PERSPECTIVE CONCEPTUALIZE POWER?

As suggested, scholars who work from the four approaches may not always agree on the central questions about information and how to intervene power structure formed by information, but they are likely to agree that power governs the production, distribution, and consumption of information (Babe, 1995; Mosco & Wasko, 1988; Schiller, 1994). Power governs social relations which give some groups more control over resources. Social relations are constituted by more than social class, gender, and race—they are also constituted by geographical locations, religions, and so on. Resources are not only about money, but they also include symbolic power and access to resources. It is unquestionable that the wealthiest individuals can use their money to acquire goods and accumulate assets, but they also have more access to influence political decisions and cultural taste than the average person.

The control over information illustrates how power works. Recalling the example about 1820s Boston: The literate populations were more likely to have control over information because they could read and provide their interpretation to others who could not. In an information-rich society with high literacy rate, information inequality has not all but disappeared. To give an example of the computing industry. History shows that the pioneers were all white males working in universities in the U.K. and the U.S. (though some of them had probably identified themselves as Jewish exiles from Europe rather than whites). Women and non-white populations outside the two countries were marginally involved in the earliest development of the Internet. In fact, the majority of the world's populations were still recovering from WWII and were more concerned with daily necessities than inventing the computer. The founders and CEOs of the most well-known information and computing companies also reflect the domination of white males from the developed world. Even though women made some gains in higher education in the U.K. and the U.S., women still tend to steer away from studying computing science (Galvin, 2016; "Why girls are put off studying computer science", 2016).

Since the 1970s, the most drastic change in the landscape of digital technology is that telecommunications and computing industries in East Asia have experienced some fast growth. Japan and South Korea are not only some of the most wired nations, but are also leaders in mobile phone and gaming technologies. China, with the largest population, has its homegrown companies such as China Mobile, Tencent (social networking), Alibaba (e-commerce), Baidu (search engine), and Xiaomi (mobile phone). While it may appear that the rise of East Asia is challenging the domination of the West, this assumption is too simplistic in conceptualizing how power works in information-rich societies, as explored in more detail below.

Power is believed to reside in stable and self-contained entities such as individuals, companies, and countries, but I argue that power is produced and distributed in networks that connect these actors (Couldry, 2008; Farias & Mützel, 2015; Galloway & Thacker, 2007; Lee, 2019; see also Davis, 2011). In other words, what made the largest information companies such as Alphabet (parent company of Google) and Baidu (the most popular search engine in the Chinese language) powerful is not because of the owners' wealth or their inventions or the countries in where they are based. They are powerful because of the formal and informal relationships between the owners, board members, venture capitalists, elite universities, and policy-makers. Take Alphabet as an example: the board members are alumni of a few top universities in the world; the company spends huge sums of money to lobby bills at different levels of government. These formal and informal relationships are intensely local but global at the same time. Most of Alphabet's networks are clustered in Silicon Valley, but they also extended to Washington DC, where Alphabet maintains a lobbying office. The networks also include regional offices in major cities around the world, and financial hubs where Alphabet stocks are traded. In this sense, stretched-out networks allow for a critique of the spatial dimension of power (Couldry, 2008). At the same time, these networks of people and money actively exclude some populations, such as temporary workers who work for Alphabet and low-income residents living in expensive tech hubs and banking centers (Sassen, 2001).

Despite the exclusivity of networks, many who live in information-rich societies may still congratulate their countries for having a competitive information sector. Low-income residents may be grateful for the spillover benefits brought by wealthy technology giants; and some temporary workers may feel proud of having a recognizable name on their resumés; successful corporations also heighten a population's national image. How to explain these positive sentiments towards the networks that actively exclude low-income residents and contract workers? Once again, one single approach could not do it all, so this book aims to show how we could answer these questions, along with many others, in the following chapters.

To conclude, critical scholars aim to examine power inequality in resource allocation and meaning-making in both information-rich and information-poor societies. They believe that end users and consumers must become critics, activists, and creators in order to see through the illusion of power equality. In the rest of the chapter, I will name four enduring issues in the study of information and provide a roadmap for readers who would take up the charge of transforming themselves from a passive to an active position.

ENDURING ISSUES IN THE STUDY OF INFORMATION

Once power is foregrounded as an analytical concept, we will see some enduring issues persist in societies, whether they are information-rich or information-poor, whether the means of communication is face to face or online. These issues manifest in different ways in different societies during different time periods. For example, information access is still unequal between boy and girl children in developing countries. More, better, and faster information will not solve this problem. We need to understand how power dictates who should receive education and who should not. In the past, "scientific" reasons that denied women's intellects were used to explain why women should not be given an education; nowadays economic reasons may explain why some families do not offer formal education to girl children. Gender inequality in education and information access can only be addressed when we take into account power that governs unequal resource allocation. If we fail to do so, this and other enduring issues about information and society will be dismissed as technical problems for which solutions are only technological. In the following, I name four enduring issues that guide the inquiry in the book. In the conclusion, we will revisit these issues and connect them with the discussion in the chapters.

Issue 1 Information Divides

Access to information—whether it is analogue (such as words of mouth) or digital (such as websites)—is not equal between classes, genders, races, ethnicities, geographical locations, ages, and so on. Divides cannot be solely explained by technological and technical limitations, but also need to be explained with economic, political, and cultural reasons (Segev, 2010; Warschauer, 2003; Youngs, 2005). For example, unreliable Internet connections in rural areas are not only due to geographical locations, but are also due to economic reasons (rural populations are seen to have less disposable income), political reluctance (governments were unwilling to provide cheap or free Internet connection), and cultural (some residents, especially the elderly, may feel they do not need to be digitally connected). Information divides cannot be solved by technological solutions because they are symptomatic of inequalities while constituting them. In other words, information divides show social and economic inequalities; not having access to information further exacerbates such inequalities.

Issue 2 Who Has the Power to Define, Control, Create, and Commodify Information?

I asserted earlier that humans and technologies both have agencies to create and reinforce digital divides. People in authority such as CEOs, religious leaders, politicians, educators, media producers, software engineers, and so on have power to shape an understanding of information. For example, college professors have the power to define "information" in class, politicians have the power to classify politically sensitive information, media workers have the power to produce information for a national audience. However, humans are not the only actors who have agency; technical devices also do. For example, wifi disruption causes loss of Internet access, the physical boundaries of newsprint limit the number of words printed on it. Power is usually seen to be negative when it is abused, but power can also be positive. In the words of Fuchs (2011), power has transformative capacity, "the capability to intervene in a given set of events so in some way to alter them" (p. 4). For example, microblogging sites allow users to share information when wifi fails, making Twitter a more effective communication means during natural disasters. Twitter is also used by activists to communicate with each other when government shuts down the Internet during civil unrest.

Issue 3 Information is Not Neutral

Because information is defined, created, controlled, and commodified by power, information is never politically, economically, and culturally neutral (Segev, 2010). I have used the example of 1820s Boston to illustrate this point. Yet, even in these days, information neutrality is commonly assumed. For example, we rarely doubt that temperature is a piece of objective information, but we also need to accept that a weather forecast is an *interpretation*. In addition, technologies are also not neutral. For example, auto-spelling correction suggests changes based on a large amount of data, but it has very low tolerance of wordplay and spelling variations.

Issue 4 Social Change and Resistance

Information divides and inequality are not new to the digital age, they certainly existed as soon as humans produced information for social survival. Changes in social ideals, however, bring awareness to information divides and their adverse effects on certain populations. For example, most populations now recognize the importance of literacy and how it relates to economic well-being and political participation, but we remain digitally illiterate by not completely understand how our online activities relate to economic and political lives. Combating mass literacy sometimes requires state effort, but activists and citizens can also bring small-scale resistance.

ROADMAP

A critical perspective that draws on political economy, critical cultural studies, feminist theories, and critical race theories will illustrate how the concept power frames the discussion of some enduring issues of information and society. To guide the readers to think about the complexity of information, this book guides them to shift their positioning from end user to critic, activist, and creator. Each of Chapters 2 to 6 is about one type of interaction between users and information.

Chapter 2, "Defining", first discusses why the word information has become more popular in the lexicon since the 1950s. We will look at how different disciplines define it. We will also look at how theorists and practitioners define information society and information economy. At the end of the chapter, I define information by relating it to time and space.

Chapter 3, "Searching", suggests that before a search, information has first to be organized. How information is organized has implications on knowledge. Humans have long organized information before the birth of search engines: dictionaries, maps, and road atlases are some organization systems that have profoundly impacted societies. To cope with an explosion of digital information, information literacy movement advocates for skills to search, evaluate, and use information.

Chapter 4, "Accessing", examines the interdependent relationship between information and technology. I assert that information bears property of technology. However, an examination of four influential communication models and the work of two international organizations show that this relationship is rarely acknowledged. Since information access is often tied to citizenry, I look at how two intellectuals explain the importance of information to citizens in the earliest 20th century. In modern discourses, good citizens are often seen as the same as good consumers.

Chapter 5, "Using", examines how organizations such as governments and corporations use information to control citizens and consumers. Even though information is said to aid governments to provide better services to citizens, the history of the U.S. census shows that information was used to advance the interests of the white race. In addition, military uses information in combat and to justify wars. Similar to governments, corporations believe that Big Data will serve consumers better, but data-driven decisions often limit consumers' choices.

Chapter 6, "Creating", examines the value of information, in particular why inexhaustive goods have such a high price tag in the market. I explain this with market structure and intellectual property. In addition, I examine who information workers are and how they make value in the market. Lastly, I examine how some artists and activists re-define the value of information through arts and alternative intellectual property arrangements.

Chapter 7, "Conclusion: Can we do more with information?", asks us to take up the positions of creators, activists, and critics to resist information produced within unequal social relations. We need to ask how we can do more with information rather than how we can cope with more information. To do more with information, we need to re-assess the value of information and exercise agency to resist unequal power relations.

BIBLIOGRAPHY

Abidin, C., & Thompson, E. (2012). Buymylife.com: Cyber-femininities and commercial intimacy in blogshops. *Women's Studies International Forum*, 35(6), 467–477.

Babe, R. E. (1995). *Communication and the transformation of economics: Essays in information, public policy, and political economy*. Boulder, CO: Westview Press.

Babe, R. E. (2010). *Cultural studies and political economy: Toward a new integration*. Lanham, MD: Rowman and Littlefield.

Braman, S. (2006). *Change of state: Information, policy, and power*. Cambridge, MA: MIT Press.

Brandom, R. (2020, May 26). Sick days: Instacart promises a safer way to shop, but workers tell a different story. *The Verge*. Retrieved from: https://www.theverge.com/21267669/instacart-shoppers-sick-extended-pay-quarantine-leave-coronavirus

Bryceson, D. F. (1985). *Women and technology in developing countries: Technological change and women's capabilities and bargaining positions.* Saint Domingo, Dominican Republic: INSTRAW.

Bunz, M., & Meikle, G. (2018). *The internet of things.* Malden, MA: Polity Press.

Burgess, J., & Green, J. (2018). *YouTube: Online video and participatory culture* (2nd ed.). Malden, MA: Polity Press.

Callon, M. (1991). Techno-economic networks and irreversibility. In J. Law (Ed.), *A sociology of monsters: Essays on power, technology and domination* (pp. 132–161). London: Routledge.

Callon, M., & Law, J. (1995). Agency and the hybrid collectif. *South Atlantic Quarterly, 94,* 481–507.

Couldry, N. (2008). After network theory and media: Do they connect and on what terms. In A. Hepp, F. Krotz, S. Moores, & C. Winter (Eds.), *Connectivity, networks and flows: Conceptualizing contemporary communication* (pp. 93–110). Creskill, NJ: Hampton Press.

Curtin, M. (2009). Matrix media. In G. Turner & J. Tay (Eds.), *Television studies after TV: Understanding television in the post-broadcast era* (pp. 13–19). New York: Routledge.

Daniels, J. (2009). *Cyber racism: White supremacy online and the new attack on civil rights.* Lanham, MD: Rowman and Littlefield.

Daniels, J. (2012). Race and racism in Internet Studies: A review and critique. *New Media and Society, 15*(5), 695–719.

Davis, A. (2011). Mediation, financialization, and the global financial crisis: An inverted political economy perspective. In D. Winseck & D. Y. Jin (Eds.), *The political economies of media: The transformation of the global media industries* (pp. 241–254). London: Bloomsbury.

Farias, I., & Mützel, S. (2015). Cultural and actor network theory. *International encyclopedia of the social and behavioral sciences* (2nd ed., Vol. 5) (pp. 523–527). Oxford: Elsevier.

Floridi, L. (2010). *Information: A very short introduction.* Oxford: Oxford University Press.

Fuchs, C. (2011). *Foundations of critical media and information studies.* London: Routledge.

Fuchs, C. (2013). Theorising and analysing digital labor: From global value chains to modes of production. *The Political Economy of Communication, 2*(1), 3–27.

Fuchs, C. (2016). *Reading Marx in the information age: A media and communication studies perspective on Capital Volume 1.* New York: Routledge.

Galloway, A. R., & Thacker, E. (2007). *Exploit: A theory of networks.* Minneapolis, MN: University of Minnesota Press.

Galvin, G. (2016, October 20). Study: Middle school is key to girls' coding interest. *US News.* Retrieved from: https://www.usnews.com/news/data-mine/articles/2016-10-20/study-computer-science-gender-gap-widens-despite-increase-in-jobs

Gamboa, S. (2020, March 19). After pressure, Trump coronavirus guide is in Spanish on CDC, White House sites. *NBC.* Retrieved from: https://www.nbcnews.com/news/latino/after-pressure-trump-coronavirus-guide-spanish-cdc-white-house-sites-n1164391

Goffey, A. (2008). Algorithm. In M. Fuller (Ed.), *Software studies: A lexicon* (pp. 15–20). Cambridge, MA: MIT Press.

Grossberg, L. (1996). The space of culture, the power of space. In I. Chambers & L. Curti (Eds.), *The post-colonial question: Common skies, divided horizons* (pp. 169–188). London: Routledge.

Halavais, A. (2017). *Search engine society* (2nd ed.). Malden, MA: Polity Press.

Hall, S. (1973). *Encoding and decoding in the television discourse*. Birmingham, UK: Centre for Contemporary Cultural Studies.

Hardt, M., & Negri, A. (1993). Postmodernization, or the informatization of production. In S. During (Ed.), *The cultural studies reader* (3rd ed.) (pp. 189–201). London: Routledge.

Hebdige, D. (1979). *Subculture: The meaning of style*. London: Routledge.

Hjorth, L., Burgess, J., & Richardson, I. (Eds.). (2012). *Studying mobile media: Cultural technologies, mobile communication, and the iPhone*. New York: Routledge.

Horkheimer, M., & Adorno, T. W. (2006). The culture industry: Enlightenment as mass deception. In M. G. Durham & D. M. Kellner (Eds.), *Media and cultural studies: Keyworks* (revised ed.) (pp. 41–72). Malden, MA: Blackwell.

Horowitz, J. M., Igielnik, R., & Kochhar, R. (2020, January 9). Most Americans say there is too much economic inequality in the U.S., but fewer than half call it a top priority. *Pew Research Center*. Retrieved from: https://www.pewsocialtrends.org/2020/01/09/most-americans-say-there-is-too-much-economic-inequality-in-the-u-s-but-fewer-than-half-call-it-a-top-priority/

Huws, U. (2003). *The making of a cybertariat: Virtual work in a real world*. New York: The Monthly Review Press.

Huws, U. (2013). Shifting boundaries: Gender, labor, and new information and communication technology. In C. Carter, L. Steiner, & L. McLaughlin (Eds.), *The Routledge companion to media and gender* (pp. 147–156). New York: Routledge.

Jang, K. (2021). Sharing, selling, striving: The gender labour of female social entrepreneurship in South Korea. In M. Lee & P. Chung (Eds.), *Media technologies for work and play in East Asia: Critical perspectives on Japan and South Koreas* (pp. 47–72). Bristol, UK: Bristol University Press.

Jenkins, H. (2009). *Confronting the challenges of participatory culture: Media education for the 21st century*. Cambridge, MA: MIT Press.

Jin, D. Y. (2015). *Digital platforms, imperialism and political culture*. London: Routledge.

John, N. (2016). *The age of sharing*. Malden, MA: Polity Press.

Kitchin, R. (2014). *Thinking critically about and researching algorithms*. The programmable city working paper 5. National University of Ireland Maynooth, County Kildare, Ireland.

Latour, B. (1993). *We have never been modern* (C. Porter trans.). Cambridge, MA: Harvard University Press.

Law, J. (1999). After ANT: Complexity, naming and topology. In J. Law & J. Hassard (Eds.), *Actor network theory and after* (pp. 1–14). Oxford: Blackwell.

Lee, M. (2019). *Alphabet: The becoming of Google*. New York: Routledge.

Lievrouw, L. A. (2014). Materiality and media in communication and technology studies. In T. Gillespie, P. J. Boczkowski, & K. A. Foot (Eds.), *Media technologies: Essays on communication, materialities, and society* (pp. 23–51). Cambridge, MA: MIT Press.

Lobato, R, (2019). *Netflix nations: The geography of digital distribution*. New York: New York University Press.

Lupton, D. (2016). *The quantified self*. Malden, MA: Polity Press.

MacKenzie, A. (2005). The performativity of code: Software and cultures of circulation. *Theory, Culture, and Society, 22*(1), 71–92.

Marx, K. (1999). *Capital: A critique of political economy*. Marxists.org. Retrieved from: https://www.marxists.org/archive/marx/works/1867-c1/ (original published in 1887).

Marx, K., & Engels, F. (2006). The ruling class and the ruling ideas. In M. G. Durham & D. M. Kellner (Eds.), *Media and cultural studies: Keyworks* (revised ed.) (pp. 9–12). Malden, MA: Blackwell.

Mattelart, A. (2003). *The information society: An introduction*. (S. G. Taponier & J. A. Cohen trans.). London: Sage.

McLaughlin, L. (2005). Cisco systems, the UN, and the corporatization of development. In G. Lovink & S. Zehle (Eds.), *Incommunicado reader* (pp. 50–63). Amsterdam: Institute of Network Cultures.

McRobbie, A. (1978). *"Jackie": An ideology of adolescent femininity*. Birmingham, UK: Centre for Contemporary Cultural Studies.

Morley, D. (1980). *The nationwide audience*. London: British Film Institute.

Mosco, V. (2004). *The digital sublime: Myth, power, and cyberspace*. Cambridge, MA: MIT Press.

Mosco, V., & Wasko, J. (Eds). (1988). *The political economy of information*. Madison, WI: The University of Wisconsin Press.

Murthy, D. (2018). *Twitter: Social communication in the Twitter age* (2nd ed.). Malden, MA: Polity Press.

Nakamura, L. (2007). *Digitizing race: Visual cultures of the internet*. Minneapolis, MN: University of Minnesota Press.

National Center for Women and Information Technology. (2007). *NCWIT Scorecard 2007: A report on the status of women in information technology*. Boulder, CO: National Center for Women and Information Technology.

Noble, S. U. (2018). *Algorithms of oppression: How search engines reinforce racism*. New York: New York University Press.

O'Carroll, A. (2008). Fuzzy holes and intangible time: Time in a knowledge industry. *Time and Society, 17*(2/3), 179–193.

Ormrod, S. (1995). Feminist sociology and methodology: Leaky black boxes in gender/technology relations. In K. Grint & R. Gill (Eds.) *The gender-technology relation: Contemporary theory and research* (pp. 31–47). London: Taylor and Francis.

Perrin, A., & Turner, E. (2019). Smartphones help blacks, Hispanics bridge some—but not all—digital gaps with whites. *Pew Research Center*. Retrieved from: https://www.pewresearch.org/fact-tank/2019/08/20/smartphones-help-blacks-hispanics-bridge-some-but-not-all-digital-gaps-with-whites/

Preda, A. (2009). *Information, knowledge and economic life: An introduction to the sociology of markets*. Oxford, UK: Oxford University Press.

Ramsey, N., & McCorduck, P. (2005). *Where are the women in information technology? Report of literature search and interviews*. Boulder, CO: The National Center for Women and Information Technology.

Robins, K. (1982). Review of the book *Who knows: Information in the age of the Fortune 500* by H. Schiller. *Media, Culture, Society*, 4(3), 298–300.

Sassen, S. (2001). *The global city: New York, London, Tokyo* (2nd ed.). Princeton, NJ: Princeton University Press.

Schiller, D. (1994). Commentary. In R. E. Babe (Ed.), *Information and communication in economics* (pp. 138–145). New York: Springer.

Schiller, D. (2007). *How to think about information*. Urbana, IL: University of Illinois Press.

Schiller, H. I. (1981). *Who knows: Information in the age of the Fortune 500*. Norwood, NJ: Ablex.

Schiller, H. I. (1989). *Culture, Inc.: The corporate takeover of public expression*. New York: Oxford University Press.

Segev, E. (2010). *Google and the digital divide: The bias of online knowledge*. Oxford: Chandes.

Simard, C. (2007). *Barriers to the advancement of technical women: A review of the literature*. Palo Alto, CA: Anita Borg Institute for Women and Technology.

Smith, E., & Reeves, R. V. (2020, September 23). Students of color most likely to be learning online: Districts must work even harder on race equity. *Brookings*. Retrieved from: https://www.brookings.edu/blog/how-we-rise/2020/09/23/students-of-color-most-likely-to-be-learning-online-districts-must-work-even-harder-on-race-equity/

Smythe, D. W. (1977). Communications: Blindspot of western Marxism. *Canadian Journal of Political and Social Theory*, 2(2), 120–127.

Sterne, J., & Stabile, C. (2003). Using women as middle men: The promise of ICTs. *Feminist Media Studies*, 3(3), 364–368.

Utz, S. (2016). Is LinkedIn making you more successful? The informational benefits derived from public social media. *New Media & Society*, 18(11), 2685–2702.

Wajcman, J., & Jones, P. K. (2012). Border communication: Media sociology and STS. *Media Culture, and Society*, 34(6), 673–690.

Warschauer, M. (2003). *Technology and social inclusion: Rethinking the digital divide*. Cambridge, MA: MIT Press.

Webster, J. (1995). What do we know about gender and information technology at work? A discussion of selected feminist research. *The European Journal of Women's Studies*, 2(3), 315–334.

"Why girls are put off studying computer science". (2016, December 23). *The Conversation*. Retrieved from: http://theconversation.com/why-girls-are-put-off-studying-computer-science-70691

Winchester, S. (2018). *The perfectionists: How precision engineers created the modern world*. New York: Harper.

Woolgar, S. (1991). Configuring the user: The case of usability trials. In J. Law (Ed.), *A sociology of monsters: Essays on power, technology, and domination* (pp. 58–99). New York: Routledge.

Youngs, G. (2005). Ethics of access: Globalization, feminism and information society. *Journal of Global Ethics*, 1(1), 69–84.

2

DEFINING

INTRODUCTION

Information is a word that we regularly use in daily lives, yet have a hard time to define what it is. There are at least three reasons to explain why this is the case: first, we cannot see information, we can only see its representation; second, the word "information" is used in a wide range of contexts in daily lives, from the very general to the very specific; third, information is used as a synonym of other terms (such as data and statistics), making the word all encompassing yet ambiguous. In the following, I first elaborate each of the three reasons before relating them to the central questions asked in this chapter.

The first reason why information is hard to define is that it is an abstract concept, not a "thing" that can be seen or touched. Images give this abstract concept a concrete "appearance", making it a tangible object. Despite its abstract nature, futuristic images that represent information share some similarities, such as cool colors, the two digits "1" and "0", human hands touching a computer, network diagrams with webs and nodes. All these images illustrate that information is digital because it is not produced by analogue technologies such as pen and paper.

The second reason why information is hard to define is that it could mean something very general or something very specific (Buckland, 2017; von Baeyer, 2004). In the broadest sense, information is recorded on a wide range of media from books, audiovisual recordings, to the Internet. In this sense, information can be numbers, words, still and moving images, sounds, or computer code; it can include something objective (such as facts) and subjective (such as opinions and feelings). In other instances, information can also be something highly specific and contextual. For example, when police seek information to solve cases, they are looking for tips that directly relate to these cases. They are not interested in subjective information such as individuals' opinions or feelings. Similarly, when visitors approach an information counter inside a hospital, they ask for directions rather than medical advice. When information is broad and specific at the same time, how do we understand the word when it is used?

The third reason why information is hard to define is that it is a synonym of many other concepts. The Oxford English Dictionary lists the following:

- details, particulars, facts, figures, statistics, data;
- knowledge, intelligence;
- instruction, advice, guidance, direction, counsel, enlightenment;
- news, notice, word;
- material, documentation, documents.

Some of these synonyms refer to numbers, others written and spoken words. Some refer to high-level analysis, others raw data. Some refer to objective information, others contextual. Reinforcing an earlier point, what information means depends on the context in which the word is used.

If the definition of "information" is all encompassing and context-dependent, then why does the definition matter? It matters because the definition of an abstract concept shapes how we see the world. For example, concepts such as "democracy", "freedom", and "love" give us meanings about life and hopes. However, unlike these concepts that may elicit strong feelings from us, we may feel neutral towards that of "information". The neutrality of information makes it appear to be an inevitable part of life. However, this apparent neutrality hides the process in which the concept actively shapes our worldview, such as our senses of time and space which in return shape our gender, racial, and class relations with others.

How does an apparently neutral concept shape our worldwide? Let us go back to the images that we found when we Googled "information". These images overwhelmingly show a futuristic world in which fair-skinned males control information and technology. The use of cool tones—blue, black, and white colors—implies information lives in the future, not the past. In this space, networks of humans and machines "float" in space and are not anchored in any geographical locales (such as countries) or locations (such as the office). The webs show that human–human connections are as important as human–machine connections. However, humans are the primary actors who exercise agency to initiate connections. Interaction with information is shown to be effortless: only a light touch on the keyboard or an extension of the hand will do. These images are nothing but neutral, they show a bias in space, time, and social relations: information occupies a space of flows (Castells, 2004), its worldview is future-oriented, and humans are the primary actors.

Not only are these images biased in space, time, and relation, they are also gender-, race-, and class-biased. The hand that initiates the interaction belongs to a white male of the professional class. Rarely do the hands belong to women, people of color, elderly people, or manual laborers. If the representation of information is not neutral, then we should question why the concept of information elicits neutrality. To explore this further, we will focus on four big questions in this chapter.

Why Has Information Received More Public Attention Since the Mid-20th Century?

Information urgently needs a definition because it has gained currency since the mid-20th century. Even though humans have shared information through sounds, words, images, and nonverbal signs for a very long time (Floridi, 2010), the word "information" had not been widely used until there was a pervasive use of digital and computing technologies in the general population in the 1950s. The rise of digital technology, like information, is not neutral; it needs to be contextualized in the history of the U.S. military. Because of this origin, how does it shape the definition of information?

How Is Information Defined in Different Disciplines?

As suggested, the definition of information is all-encompassing yet context-specific. How do scholars in different fields define the concept? I will examine how the disciplines of communication, biology, mathematics, and library sciences define it by finding out the similarities and differences between them. I will them ask how these similarities, differences, and limitations inform the assumed neutrality of the concept. Lastly, I will ask how this assumed neutrality can be critiqued from the lenses of race.

What Are Information Society and Information Economy?

The futuristic images of information illustrate a belief that information brings in a new type of society known as an information society. Does an information society mark a dramatic break from the past or is it simply old wine in a new bottle? In other words, is society organized differently because of information and computing technologies, or is it more or less the same? An information society is also believed to bring in a new kind of economy, which would bring unprecedented growth to a country. How does an assumed neutrality of information promote a new kind of society and economy?

What Is the Relationship Between Information, Time, and Space?

As previously shown, images that represent information take place in an undefined space in a future-oriented world. It is unknown whether information is created in an existing space and time or whether information creates time and space. If the latter is true, then those who have the power to create information also have an opportunity to create our senses of time and space, which in turn shape our worldview. In this last section, I will draw on the definitions of information from the disciplines of molecular biology and library science to show how these disciplines create time and space for practitioners and the general public.

Readers may notice that I have yet to define information. I will take up this challenging task at the end of the chapter.

WHY HAS INFORMATION RECEIVED MORE ATTENTION SINCE THE MID-20TH CENTURY?

The word "information" came from late Middle English (1400–1500 AD) and has a Latin origin. According to Oxford dictionary, the Latin word "informatio" derives from the verb "informare" which means "to form, mould, fashion, give shape to", "delineate, sketch, form an idea", or "inform, instruct, educate". These meanings still apply to what we mean by "to inform" in today's context. For example, evidence "informs" an argument, teachers "inform" students.

Despite the word has existed since the 1400s, it has gained more popularity since 1920. To illustrate this, I used Ngram Viewer of Google Books to illustrate how frequent the word "information" appeared in English-language books between 1800 and 2000. The frequency was stable from 1800 to 1920 but increased by 72 percent from 1920 to 1960 and 138 percent from 1960 to 2000.

Google Books give some ideas how the meaning of "information" has been changing since 1920 and why there has been a surge of usage since early 1990s. There are only five scanned books from the year 1920 with the word "information" in the title: one is an index of published articles, some others are information about Russia, refrigeration, and the American Red Cross.

One title that well illustrates a 1920s understanding of information was a report about U.S. propaganda effort during WWI. The report was submitted to the President by the Chairman of the Committee on Public Information (Committee on Public Information, 1920). It stated that influencing public opinion is very important to win the war so the Committee aimed to "make the fight for loyalty and unity at home, and for the friendship and understanding of the neutral nations of the world" (p. 13). The committee shared these messages through daily war news, speeches, advertising, pamphlets, public arts, plays, movies, photographs, and newspapers. The committee not only influenced U.S. public opinion, but also the international one by broadcasting its messages to Europe, Latin America, and Asia. The committee believed that these messages have changed various countries' attitudes towards the United States, changing it from a foe to a friend. Even though what it did is clearly what we call propaganda nowadays, the committee refused to see itself as a propaganda machine. The word "information" shows the committee's belief in neutral information.

Google Books has scanned 18 books published in 1960 the titles of which contain the word "information". The nature of some of these books was similar to those published in the year 1920; they provided facts and statistics about specialized information such as Nigeria forestry, aviation, statistics of British colonies, and attitudes of U.S. army officers. However, some titles reflected an emerging discipline of information science, such as information management and processing. These books were published by university presses, international organizations, and U.S. agencies. The titles may show that while information was seen to be the same as facts, it also needs to be organized and managed for different purposes.

According to Google Books, in 2000, there was an explosion of books with the word "information" in the title. Unlike those in the years 1920 and 1960, almost all of these publications were academic books. Few of them offered facts and statistics, probably because the Internet could deliver more updated field-specific information than books. Some books contribute to the discipline of information science such as information systems, knowledge management, information security management, computing, cybersecurity; others examined how information has transformed society, culture, and economy. These titles show that information has become subjects of academic inquiries more than collections of facts and statistics.

The Development of Information Science

The book titles discussed above show that information science has gained more attention from scholars since the 1960s, so it is worthwhile to examine why information science became a discipline. In particular, why did scholars and practitioners feel there is a need to study the organization and management of information?

Herner (1984) suggested that the discipline began well before 1960s; it began as a convergence of "library science, computer science [...], documentation of research and development, abstracting, indexing, communications science, behavioral science, micro- and macro-publishing, and video and optical science" (p. 157). Prior to 1945, there was more documentation about library science than information science (Buckland & Liu, 1998).

1945 was the unofficial year when the discipline of information science commenced (Herner, 1984; Saracevic, 1992), marked by American engineer Vannevar Bush's highly influential article "As we may think" (1945) published in *The Atlantic*. Bush played a paramount role in military research and development during WWII. In this article, he argued that the conclusion of the war should not slow down scientists' quest to advance information technology for civilian use. He envisioned an earlier form of the Internet: "Memex" was imagined as an encyclopedia from which users can consult any knowledge.

In the 1950s and 1960s, information science encompassed more professions who engaged in a wide range of activities. The primary professional society for information scientists, the Association for Information Science and Technology (ASIS&T) stated that its members have expanded their interest beyond documentation; they began to investigate how automatic services can aid literature searching, information storage and retrieval. These activities then probed investment in the information industry (Saracevic, 1992).

In the 1960s, ASIS&T further expanded the scope of information science to include designing, managing, and using information systems and technology. In the same decade, the first textbook *Information storage and retrieval* (Becker & Hayes, 1963) was published, solidifying information science as a discipline. In the same year, the President's Science Advisory Committee commissioned a high-profiled report *Science, Government, and Information* (Science Advisory Committee, 1963). These activities seemed to reflect Vannevar Bush's call for an investment in information technology by carrying out large-scaled, well-funded and organized activities (Saracevic, 1992).

In the 1970s, information scientists adopted a more encompassing view of information. For example, Goffman (1970; cited in Saracevic, 1992) advocated for a unified scientific approach to study information related to biological processes, human existence, and the machines. In the mid-1970s, information scientists also called attention to the role that humans play to create, use, and communicate information. For example, Saracevic (1992) redefined information science as a field to study how humans effectively communicate and record knowledge to fulfill social, institutional, and individual needs.

The advancement of information and communication technologies can account for a redefinition of information science in the 1970s when there was a shift from mini and micro computers to more powerful mainframe computers, making formerly distinct disciplines become interdisciplinary because mainframe computers can process more information in a shorter timeframe. Furthermore, in the 1980s, individual users can access online databases from their personal computer. They no longer needed to rely on expensive equipment. In the new millennium, ASIS&T started to pay attention to the social implications of the pervasive use of information and communication technology, in particular social consequences of online databases in the industry, the government and education.

The development of the information science discipline mirrors books about information scanned by Google. In the first half of the 20th century, information was about facts and statistics. Since 1960s, the advancement of technologies led to the creation of applications that create, organize, and retrieve information. Since the 1980s, the pervasive use of information technologies probed scholars to study the social impact of information. So far, information appears to be monolithic; in the next section we will look at how different disciplines conceptualize it in different ways.

HOW IS INFORMATION DEFINED IN DIFFERENT DISCIPLINES?

Von Baeyer (2004) suggested that information is the key to understand diverse principles from thermodynamics to biology. Information is studied in paradigms from humanities to social sciences, from human sciences to natural sciences (Parry, 2004). We will look at how four—communication, library and information science, biology, and mathematics—conceptualize it. I chose them because they are distinct: communication is a hybrid field grounded in both humanities and social science, aiming to understand how humans communicate in both mediated and non-mediated settings, through the media and in person. Library science is an applied field that studies how to manage libraries and disseminate knowledge. Biology is a natural science that studies life and living organisms. Lastly, mathematics is a study of abstract knowledge upon which built the studies of natural, physical and applied sciences. As will be shown, scholars in these disciplines believe information solve many problems but they would also bring some more.

A Mathematics Model of Communication

Communication is a hybrid field that is grounded in both humanities and social sciences. Rhetoricians since the time of Aristotle have long asked how ethos, logos, and pathos can be used to make persuasive speeches. While these questions are still asked about political speeches and advertising copies, the pervasiveness of mass media at the turn of the 20th century had probed social scientists to examine communication as a cognitive, psychological process that has profound impact on a mass society.

The mathematical model of communication proposed by Shannon and Weaver has greatly influenced generations of communication scholars. In this model, communication is a transmission of information from the sender to the receiver: "the information source, the starting point of communication, forms the message, which is transformed into 'information' by the transmitter, which codifies it and sends it on to the other end of the chain" (Mattelart & Mattelart, 1998, p. 44). Information can be any words, sounds, or even images as long as they can be transformed into signals—at that time, electronic—that are transmitted through a medium. Shannon and Weaver, working on behalf of a telephone company, were particularly interested in the transmission of sounds through copper wires. This model can also be applied to digital information transmitted through optical fibers.

Library and Information Science

Library and information scientists design and develop knowledge-organization systems, create advisory resources and locate them. They serve the public, students and scholars, as well as professionals ("What is library and information science?", n/a). Since information and knowledge are objects of studies, it is worthwhile to see how they are defined. According to the *Online dictionary for library and information science* (Reitz, n/a), information can be defined as:

> Data presented in readily comprehensible form to which meaning has been attributed within the context of its use. In a more dynamic sense, the message conveyed by the use of a medium of communication or expression. Whether a specific message is *informative* or not depends in part on the subjective perception of the person receiving it.
>
> More concretely, all the facts, conclusions, ideas, and creative works of the human intellect and imagination that have been communicated, formally or informally, in any form. In his inaugural address of 1801, Thomas Jefferson listed the "diffusion of information" as one of the fundamental principles of the republican form of government established under the Constitution of the United States.

The above definition of information emphasizes the role that humans play in making information comprehensible and relevant. Information can be both objective—such as facts—and subjective—such as creative works. It further highlights the role that information plays in a democracy.

The same source defines knowledge as "processed" information: "information that has been comprehended and evaluated in the light of experience and incorporated into the knower's intellectual understanding of the subject" (Reitz, n/a). Knowledge then refers to a narrower range of information that involves a knower's deliberate attempt to understand unprocessed information. This knower also needs to have enough experience and adequate intellect to produce relevant knowledge.

Molecular Biology

Biologists began to incorporate the vocabulary of information and codes in the 1940s (Mattelart & Mattelart, 1998). The discoveries of DNA, the double helix, genetic codes, and later the genome have ignited public imagination that living organisms contain codes and these codes transmit from one generation to another. In 1994, Erwin Schrödinger wrote *What is life?*, in which he described chromosomes as the hereditary code-script that dictates how every individual

DEFINING 37

develops and functions in a mature state. The chromosomes were said to be the full code that will be copied when an egg fertilizes (Dronamraju, 1999). In 1944, Oswald Avery and his colleagues discovered that DNA is the material that make up genes and chromosomes. DNA makes up all organisms. What differentiates one from others is merely the composition of the four bases (A, G, C, & T). In 1953, James Watson and Francis Crick showed that the DNA molecule exists in the form of a three-dimensional double helix made up of these four bases (Moody, 2004; Pray, 2008). The double helix is called an amazing structure, an elegant "information molecule DNA" that connects one living organism to others because all organisms use this same structure to convey such information (Collins, n/a a, para. 1). The genome, lastly, is seen as a secret manual that makes up all living organisms. The genome was said to be "the entire instruction set of an organism; all of the DNA. For humans, that amounts to about 3.1 billion letters of the code—As, Cs, Gs, and Ts—all in the right order, spread across all of those chromosomes" (Collins, n/a b, para. 1). Genomes unlock the relationships between all living organisms. For example, genome comparison shows that the closest relatives of humans are the chimpanzees, they share perfect identity with 96 percent of the DNA sequence (Spencer, 2005). Genome also reveals relationships between individuals of a species. For example, commercial genome mapping services enable customers to build their family trees and to find out their racial and ethnic compositions.

In molecular biology, genes bear information. This information will be imprinted on the future generation, it also record our history. In the words of von Baeyer (2004), the genome is seen as "a code for transmitting the form of the molecular constituents of the human body from generation to generation, and gene expression is the act of in-forming—of giving form to—the atoms that serve as raw materials" (p. 151). This information embedded in genome, however, is hidden. A layperson however has access to cheap genome-mapping services to unlock the "secret" of life.

Mathematics of Information

Shannon and Weaver's mathematics model of communication has impacted the field of communication as much as the studies of the physical world. This model drew on the physical concept "entropy", which refers to the physical quantity of information, similar to that of mass or energy (Floridi, 2010; Gleick, 2011). For example, the process of the sun melting ice is a question of entropy. If entropy remains unchanged, then the process is reversible. Water can become ice if it is put in a freezer.

However, some processes are irreversible and they are to be avoided. Information was seen to be the key to avoid entropy. Nobert Wiener, teacher of Shannon, suggested that information would help organize society to avoid the entropy stage. This stage is undesirable because of "nature's tendency to destroy what is ordered and precipitate biological deterioration and social disorder" (Mattelart & Mattelart, 1998, p. 50). To avoid such disorder, he proposed to use machines to measure the degree of disorganization so that humans can use information to save themselves.

The field of mathematics of information was made possible by powerful computers that process a large quantity of information. Some mathematicians have begun to see mathematics as the language of data. They differentiate data from information. The former is about "values of qualitative or quantitative variables", the latter "the content and meaning present in data" (Schönlieb, 2017, para. 2). In other words, powerful computers can find out the limitations of data and can estimate what information can be extracted in a predicted time frame.

How do physical sciences relate to the field of mathematics? Mathematics has long been seen as an abstract language that has no bearing on the physical world. While mathematical fields such as algebra and geometry have aided scientific and engineering inquiries about logical and statistical quantities, the emerging field of the mathematics of information has a direct interest in physical quantities such as energy and temperature (Center for the Mathematics of Information, n/a). It aims to study information and computation across disciplines, from statistics and probability; applied, pure and computational analysis; to the theory and modelling of complex, dynamical, and physical systems (PhD in mathematics of information, n/a).

Communication, library science, molecular biology and a mathematics of information appear to be disparate disciplines, but Shannon and Weaver's mathematics model of communication connect them by seeing information as a physical entity that can be discovered, examined, and manipulated (García-Sancho, 2006; Parry, 2004; Thacker, 2006). To Shannon and Weaver, the goal of a mathematics model of communication was to transmit the most accurate information in the most economical way. To molecular biologists, their goal is to map out the information hidden in all living organisms (Kay, 2000; Nelkin & Lindee, 1995). To mathematics of information, the goal is to extract information from data. Lastly, the metaphors used to talk about biology are drawn from languages in human communication (Ritchie, 2004). These disciplines have profoundly impacted how humans organize themselves: from talking to each other through the telephone to finding a book from a database to diagnosing heredity diseases to automatically analyzing digital images. However, since these disciplines harbor the view that information can be extracted, measured, and compared, they may mask unequal power relations in their applications.

Even though it is hard to offer a blanket critique of how power works through social relation in the applications of information, here I offer an anecdote. 23andMe is a company that offers consumer-grade test kits to find out an individual's ancestry, including in which parts of the world their ancestors lived. However, the company has a limited database for any race other than Caucasians. A journalist who self-identifies as ethnic Korean found out that 23andMe has fewer than 100 Korean sample genes, even though there are about 80 million Koreans living in the world (Hong, 2016). The company also has many fewer African sample genes than Caucasian ones (Marcus, 2020). As a result, customers who self-identity as non-white will find the result to be much less meaningful because of racial bias of an apparently scientific genome-mapping service.

INFORMATION SOCIETY AND INFORMATION ECONOMY

In the previous sections, I have shown that since the 1960s, there have been more academic studies about information; in addition, some disciplines see information as a physical entity that can be measured and observed. Both provide a condition for scholars and practitioners to wonder if an information-saturated society is a new kind of society. If it is, then what should we call it and what role does information play in it? We will examine three ways to conceptualize an information-rich society: a post-industrial society, a network society, and an information economy.

Information Society

The premise of an information society is that the pervasive use of information and communication technologies has brought large-scaled and unprecedented change to every facet of society. This change has drastically transformed economy, politics, and the everyday life (see Webster, 2006 for critique). This change is also believed to be irreversible: once a society has moved to this new stage, it is not likely to go back to the previous stage. This change is also believed to be universal, that all countries—regardless of their political system and development stage—would embrace such a change. Daniel Bell and Manuel Castells are two scholars who have theorized this new society.

Writing in the mid-1970s, Daniel Bell (1973) believed that developed countries are moving towards a post-industrial society. A post-industrial society is the third and final stage of all societies. The first stage is an agrarian society where the main production is food. This kind of society requires a lot of intensive labour power, land, and raw resources (such as water). All human societies began as agricultural societies, but some developing countries are deemed to be agricultural societies as well.

The second stage is an industrial society. In this society, machines are used to mass produce commodities from clothing to household items to automobiles. The industrial revolution that took place in Britain in the mid-1800s is commonly seen as the starting point of this kind of society. Many developing countries are now in this stage. These societies tend to have cheap labor cost and land for factories. This kind of society also requires a lot of labor power but raw resources can be shipped from other places. Unlike production in an agricultural society where output is slow, inconsistent, and unpredictable, production in an industrial society can produce a large number of identical products in a steady speed. In addition, laborers in an agrarian society cannot transfer their knowledge from one place to another place, but those in an industrial society could transfer some knowledge from one factory to another.

The third stage is a post-industrial society. In this stage, the computer has replaced all machines in all stages of production: from planning a product, making it, and selling it in the market. This post-industrial society first appeared in the 1970s in developed societies in Western Europe, North America, and some parts of Asia Pacific. These countries tend to have a highly educated workforce, a lot of know-how, knowledge, and a concentration of capital (Webster, 2006). The post-industrial society tends to produce intangible goods such as information, knowledge, and services more than tangible goods such as consumer goods. Knowledge is believed to have replaced capital and labor as the decisive factor of production (Schiller, 1988). The types of goods and services vary a lot. For example, intellectual property of software share little commonalities with retail services. To produce software, it takes a number of highly paid engineers with very specialized knowledge. To sell a computer, it does not take too many highly paid employees to learn the ropes. Despite this, laborers in a post-industrial society generally need some specialized knowledge acquired from years of formal schooling and on-the-job training. However, unlike laborers in an industrial society, this knowledge can be transferable to different jobs and industries. For example, all entry-level office workers are required to know simple word processing; this basic computing skill is applicable in a law firm as much as a medical office. In another example, software engineers who know different programming languages can find jobs in an online retailer as much as an aviation company.

What differentiates the three stages of society is not so much the changes in technology, culture, economy, or occupation, but how theoretical knowledge and information are used to conduct the everyday life (Webster, 2006). In other words, it is the quality, not quantity of information, that has ushered in a post-industrial society. To Daniel Bell, the application of theoretical knowledge would drastically change social structure; and he included the economy, the occupational structure, and social stratification system as part of social structure (Webster, 2006). To put it in simpler term, a post-industrial society differs from other societies in terms of how society and economy are organized as a result of knowledge and information.

Even though the three stages of society may describe the transformation of society, it should also be noted that not all agricultural jobs are labor-intensive. Nowadays, farmers use information technologies and machineries to plan work. On the other hand, not every service job that requires the use of information technology requires workers to have specialized knowledge. For example, restaurants may use wireless handheld devices to send food orders from the dining room to the kitchen but the servers only need very rudimentary computing skills to master the device (Poynter & de Miranda, 2000).

Network Society

Daniel Bell was not the only theorist who ponders upon the nature of this new society. Manuel Castells offered a trilogy called *The information age: Economy, society and culture* (2010) to theorize how a new kind of society organizes itself around networks. While networks are commonly understood as those on social media these days, Castells envisioned such a network before social media became popular. He believed that technologies make these networks possible through the sharing and managing of information. The constant flow of information is paramount to the maintenance of such network society. The main source of productivity in such a society relies on how knowledge acts upon knowledge (Webster, 2006). Similar to Bell, who believed that knowledge ushered in a new kind of society, Castells suggested that networks have transformed how economy, work, and culture are organized.

An information economy is necessary for a network society because a firm's success depends on its harnessing information and technologies to access networks. To give an example, the online retail giant Amazon allows vendors from other countries to sell their products to U.S. customers. To tap into the U.S. market, firms in other countries need to have access to reliable Internet and computing technologies. They also need to apply knowledge about the U.S. market to know the demand and taste of U.S. customers. In addition, they need to describe their products in English. Lastly, they will need to rely on reliable postal services to send their goods overseas. This process may sound straightforward, but it relies on multiple functioning networks, including the Internet, cultural knowledge, and postal services. Vendors that have access to these networks have a better chance to succeed at tapping into an overseas market than those who have little access to these networks.

A network society and an informational economy demand more knowledge workers than manual workers. Knowledge workers are not restricted to one job, one company, and one industry. The ability to apply knowledge to make decisions is a transferable skill across different industries. For workers who only have knowledge about one type of work, they risk being unemployed once the firm closes down when the industry is in decline. For example, many manual laborers (such as steel workers) in developed countries found they were out of a job once the goods could be produced more cheaply in other countries. The skills of these workers are not transferable. The only jobs left in the market are service jobs that tend to be unstable, pay less, and offer no job benefits. The rise of the network society does not benefit everyone. Regardless of geographical locations, younger and more educated populations are more connected to networks than older and less educated populations.

Information Economy

Both Daniel Bell and Manuel Castells are sociologists, so their primary interest is how knowledge and networks would bring changes to the society, which includes the economy. Both thinkers did not see the economy as a self-contained entity or the sole driving force of societal change. In other words, they would not agree that the economy is an insulated entity that has no relation to society and culture. However, there are definitely thinkers who believe that an information economy is a self-contained entity that can be measured. For example, the Organisation for Economic Co-operation and Development (OECD) is keen on quantifying what an information economy is.

The member-states of OECD consist of mostly developed economies in Europe and North America. Despite not all countries belong to the OECD, the organization aims to set international standards that foster prosperity, equality, opportunity, and well-being for the world's populations. It privileges economic solutions to all kinds of problems; and it prefers data-driven decisions.

OCED stated that the information economy has been growing since 2000. The use of communication networks and digital technologies will increase economic output and productivity (Babe, 1995; "Information and communication technology", n/a). To measure the size of the information economy, it collects data such as ICT employment, investment, and exports. OCED names a wide range of industries that contribute to an information economy, such as manufacture of computer, electronic and optical productions; publishing and broadcasting industries, telecommunications, computer programming, and information service activities. An information economy that includes a wide range of activities from producing and selling goods and services, hardware and software, digital information, and media entertainment. Because the information economy is so encompassing, some of the workers may produce high-value knowledge, others may be in dead-end sales jobs.

Even though Daniel Bell and Manuel Castells may not agree with OECD that an information economy can be insulated from the larger society, some of OECD's beliefs confirm the existence of a post-industrial society and network society. For example, it highlighted that information could change the workings of science, governments, and cities; technologies make certain jobs obsolete but also create new jobs; also, workers need to adapt to new skills to succeed in such a society (OECD, 2017). As suggested, even though OEDC showed its support of an information economy, not all workers are winners.

Concluding this section, I have shown that the concepts "post-industrial society", "network society", and "information economy" all point to a belief that societies of developed economies have moved to a new terrain. These societies may find it impossible to return to an earlier stage. Therefore, it is inevitable that all societies will become an information society one day. For those societies that are not yet information-rich, they should better prepare for it rather than resisting it. In the next section, I argue that this belief has a few fallacies if we take into account the relationship between information, time, and space.

INFORMATION, TIME, AND SPACE

So far I have not defined what information means. I therefore want to show in this section that understanding information requires an understanding of time and space (Hassan, 2008). Information is always produced, distributed, and consumed in a specific time and space. However, time and space change during these processes. Therefore, I do not see time and space as something fixed and unchanged. Instead, the production, distribution, and consumption of information create a new sense of time and space.

What are senses of time and space? Different societies experience time differently: some societies like to measure and quantify it; others see it as more fluid. Some societies are future-oriented, others are past-oriented. Similarly, different societies experience space differently: physical places are essential for some societies for human interactions, others less so; some societies have strict rules about who can use certain space, others are more flexible. Why spatiality—the sense of space—and temporality—the sense of time—matter in defining information is because they influence how we imagine and manage information. As I have shown in the beginning of the chapter, images that represent information have limited imagination; these limited imagination in turn limits our imagination of what information could be. How will we see information differently if there are a variety of representation that shows it has different temporalities and spatialities?

In the following, I first explain how information creates time and space, then I will examine how the definitions of information in molecular biology and library science create specific senses of temporality and spatiality for the general public. I argue that the concept information economy does the same. These senses of time and space are not neutral, they are gendered and racialized. To imagine information differently, we need to imagine other senses of time and space experienced by a wider range of people.

How Does Information Create Time and Space?

Recalling the subway commute example that opens this book, I want us to ride the subway train with other passengers again. The train time table and map provide objective information about train schedule and where the train travels. As suggested, the timetable objectifies time, making it to be something measurable. As I will show in Chapter 3, "Searching", the map externalizes memory. It aids human beings to geographically orient themselves. Despite the time schedule and map being objective, each passenger inside the train has different senses of time and space. To those who travel the same route at about the same time, they may engage with a smartphone to pass the time. Time spent on the subway is something dispensable to a regular commuter so the information on the phone helps them psychologically shorten time and transport their minds elsewhere. Those who travel the route for the first time may pay more attention to the map because it orients where they are. To tourists, a subway train ride is always exciting because every moment during the journey seems to be something new. They want to take in the physical experience as much as possible, particularly where there are views outside the train windows.

If we are to survey how different passengers experience information, time, and space in a subway train, we are likely to have a range of answers. However, if we are to ask them how molecular biology, library science, and an information economy use information to create time and space, they may be puzzled by the question. In the following, I will explain what this question means.

The Sense of Time and Space in Molecular Biology, Library Science, and the Information Economy

Let us first consider biology. Before the microscope, humans could only see what their naked eyes allow them to. The invention of the microscope confirmed the existence of microorganisms such as bacteria. Knowing that there are microorganisms allowed humans to imagine a new dimension of time and space: that these microorganisms can reproduce over time and that they live on our skin and inside our body.

The informationization of biology did the same thing to our imagination of time and space (Haraway, 1997; Waldby, 2000). The three-dimensional model of the double helix shows what our human eyes cannot see: two twisting ribbons that are connected by tiny bars. This visual representation of a DNA molecule allows humans to imagine an invisible, tiny unit inside our body, expanding our sense of space. The double helix also asks us to re-consider the formation of all living organisms and the connection between humans and other living organisms. These connections also expand space because our bodies are no longer a stand-alone entity that bears no relationship to other humans and living organisms, but one small part in the entity of all living organisms. In short, the double helix has established a network of living organisms. The bodies are re-imagined to be codes and information (Chow-White, 2008; García-Sancho, 2006).

The discovery of genome and DNA sequencing technology also create a new sense of time. Genome is likened to be a secret code embedded in each organism; this code instructs how a body should be reproduced. This secret code helps connect the present to the past, mapping a genealogy of where our ancestors came from and where our blood-related distant relatives reside. This code also gives us a sense of inevitability, that our offspring cannot escape from the present because we pass along our secret code to them. In this sense, genome and DNA sequencing favor a linear temporality where the past leads to the present and the future.

In the case of library science, the field information science renders physical space irrelevant. Knowledge used to be housed in a physical space, now knowledge is seen to be in the Internet. The Great Library of Alexandria that was founded in 285 BC had the ambition to collect all knowledge in the form of written words. The library had then been seen as a tomb of knowledge where patrons consult books and other print materials (see Chapter 6, "Creating", about the U.S. Library of Congress). The digital age has changed how space is seen in the library: instead of merely collecting physical copies of books, libraries moved them off-site. New space was crafted out for computer stations where patrons can search for online knowledge. The job of the librarians has also changed: in addition to acquiring and categorizing books, now they help users navigate the immense amount of online information. Nowadays, librarians are also information literacy instructors: not only do they teach users the tools to search for information, but they also teach them how to evaluate information (see Chapter 3, "Searching", about information literacy).

The information economy is often seen as a "new" economy, an economy of the future. As discussed in the previous section, a post-industrial society was said to be a third, if not final, stage (Bell, 1973). In this post-industrial society, Bell believed that knowledge has replaced capital to be the most valuable resource (Schiller, 1988). The OECD also believed that countries that refuse to take big strides to match towards the information economy will lag behind others Therefore, it has been playing an instrumental role to aid member-states to take that step.

The OECD publishes statistics about the information economy of different countries. For example, it compared how different countries fare in different areas in *Measuring the digital transformation: A roadmap for the future* (2019). The top five countries where information industries add value to the economy are Israel, Ireland, South Korea, Sweden, and the U.S. The worst performing countries in this aspect are Chile, Russia, New Zealand, Turkey, and South Africa. When an economy can be quantified, countries can be compared. Countries that score high in the information index means they are more future-oriented than those that score low. Those that have high scores may attract more domestic and foreign investment than those who have low scores. For those that score low, governments may need policies to improve their information sectors or else they will further lag behind. A comparison of an information economy also flattens space (Friedman, 2005). Geographical, historical, and cultural specificities of countries are rendered irrelevant when any country is believed to be able to enter the race of an information society. To give an example, Israel, Sweden, and South Korea are three of the five countries with a robust information economy, but each of these countries decided to become an information society under different historical and economic circumstances. In addition, an information society may also impact gender relations differently. A mere comparison will not reveal how different populations understand and benefit from an information society differently.

The above three examples show the definition of information shapes our senses of time and space, albeit not in the same way. Each of the three cases help us visualize space and imagine the past and the future. In the cases of the double helix and genome, information about the genes helps us visualize a "secret" code that dictates genetic composition, thus linking us from the past to the future. Digital information transforms the physical space of a library, making prints obsolete. Lastly, an information economy asks us to look into the future and disregard the past. An index about an information economy reveals how ready different countries are about the future; this comparison also erases spatial differences by making countries compete on the same plane.

Gender and Race Bias

I have shown in the previous section that information creates new senses of time and space. Why is it important to understand temporality and spatiality of information? I argue in this section that this understanding shapes that of race and gender. There are two ways in which it is done. First, a linear sense of temporality supports an assumption that something stays unchanged throughout human history; this linearity stabilizes relations between gender and race. Second, information externalizes subjective knowledge, disembedding the knowledge from the knowers (Zaloom, 2003); knowledge that is produced in a localized setting is deemed less relevant. However, objective information has gender and race bias and these biases often go unexamined.

To illustrate how information creates time and space that could be gender- and race-biased, I re-visit the examples of genome mapping and an information economy. At present, a number of companies offer genome sequencing services. One benefit is that it helps individuals make better health decisions: they will know their risk of certain diseases and side effects of medication. The belief is that human genes reproduce in the void of the outer environment even though outer environment significantly alters one's health outlook. To give an example, the major illnesses that kill Americans are related to obesity. Yet, their ancestors were much less likely to be obese, so heart disease and diabetes were not the leading causes of death. Genome sequencing will also not tell African Americans that they are at a higher risk of obesity due to poor access to healthcare and healthy food (Petersen, Pan, & Blanck, 2019). In short, knowing one's genome sequencing will not significantly change the political economic structure of why some demographics are allocated with fewer resources. Genome sequencing can foster gene essentialism that "reduces the self to a molecular entity, equating human beings, in all their social, historical, and moral complexity, with their genes" (Nelkin & Lindee, 1995, p. 2).

Some genome sequencing services market itself as a tool to find out about ancestry. For example, 23andMe promises to show customers family trees and migration history. The company believes that genome transcends time, letting customers "trace your path back thousands of years" ("Ancestry and traits service", n/a). With this new tool, some customers discovered family secrets and long-lost siblings (Collman, 2018). Genome mapping re-inscribes the notion of family being blood-related. This kind of family excludes adoptive families and same-sex parents. Even though the laws in some countries recognize the rights of same-sex and adoptive families, a biological notion of family harbors a narrow definition of a family.

Genome sequencing also has implications on race by simply describing where one's ancestors *might* come from without providing a context why ancestors migrated (or forced migrated) and what historical force was in play for the migrations. For example, slavery broke up families, erased individuals' history, and sexually violated bodies of men and women in slavery. While genome mapping may help descendants of slaves discover from which countries their ancestors came from, it did not reveal *the lives* of their ancestors (Marcus, 2020). In one example, famed African American TV host Oprah Winfrey underwent genome sequencing and found out her ancestors came from three different parts in Africa, and that she was 8 percent Native American and 3 percent Asian (Lang, 2014). This discovery, beyond the surprise factor, has not helped the public understand under what conditions were her ancestors forced to migrate to the New World, how Africa was divided into "countries", and how African Americans came into interaction with Native Americans and Asians (see Chapter 5, "Using", about how the U.S. census categorized race). Knowing one's genome may be the first step to find out about one's genealogy but by no means does genealogy mean family history. Chow-White (2008) warned that "the convergence of changing concepts of race with information technologies has produced a new paradigm of race" (p. 1169). To him, the Human Genome project redefined racial knowledge by orienting it around the digital cultures of communication technologies.

While molecular biology promotes a linear temporality that assumes the past connects to the present, library science and an information economy create a new spatiality in which digital information is believed to live free in cyberspace. Users who are able to harness digital information in this new space will have a better chance to create economic value for themselves and their countries in the "real" world. At the beginning of the chapter, I showed that those who are able to harness digital information are fair-skinned younger men. These biased images not only exclude female and non-white populations, but they also visualize objective knowledge—in this case digital information—as existing external to human beings. In this cyber world, the knowledge that is the most valuable is that external to humans. For example, a family recipe passed down through word of mouth is not as economically valuable as a recipe found online. The former does not contribute to an information economy while the latter does.

To recap, the concept information economy suggests that countries that excel at producing and consuming digital information will have a better chance to compete in the global economy. This objective economy, however, does not capture subjective knowledge of a localized economy. To use the example of recipes again, online recipes may show a robust information economy because users have to see a number of ads before seeing the recipes. The number of users and advertising money are all data that can be collected (see Chapter 6, "Creating"). However, a family recipe has no economic value even though its knowledge is subjective, such as bearing the memory of family members and traditions.

This subjective information is often shaped by race, gender, and class. Populations who are old, illiterate, and less educated tend not to contribute to online resources. Therefore, grandma recipes are usually circulated in a family unless if the younger generation wants to share them online. In another example, recent immigrants often find jobs and community resources not by reading online information, but by interacting with other immigrants. This kind of information network—albeit not done in a cyberspace—is economically significant because it helps immigrants understand the labor market in a specific locale. This kind of subjective knowledge is not measured in the information economy because these individuals may not rely on digital information to make economic decision. However, they help populations—who are said to be not tapping into the information economy—to survive. To draw on Castell's concept of network, some populations may not tap into a digital network, but their personal networks in a "real" world help them cope with a fast-changing world.

Therefore, a critical perspective would question the time and space created by information. For example, Escobar (1999) believes that women need to transform both places and time. Since places are shaped by patriarchal domineering practices, therefore places could incarcerate women's and control them. Similarly, a presupposition of the premodern implies there is a future towards which women should strive.

CONCLUSION

Information is difficult to define. We cannot see or touch information, we can only see representations of it. Sometimes the meaning of information is highly specific, sometimes very general. The meaning of information is ambiguous as well. Depends on the context, it is a synonym of knowledge, data, or content. In addition, the concept of information appears to be neutral; it does not seem to elicit much positive or negative feeling among users.

However, this chapter has shown that there is nothing neutral about the definition of information, instead its assumed neutrality actively shapes an understanding of time and space. How we understand time and space in turn shapes how race and gender are understood. At the beginning of the chapter, I have shown that information is overwhelmingly represented by young white males. These images imply that younger white males, not women or people of color or manual laborers, have a better chance to harness information. White males initiate with information in a cyberspace and they represent the future. Therefore, the definition of information has a specific spatiality and temporality, and these senses of space and time are gender and race biased. They exclude certain populations by simply omitting their presence.

Throughout the chapter, I have shown that the development of an information-saturated society is believed to take place on a linear timeline: at the beginning of the story, there was not much information, then humans created more information and changed the society as a result. This change was reflected by the sharp increase of books with the word "information" in the titles, an expansion of professions that work on information, and an expansion of an information economy. The increase in the quantity of information probed scholars to investigate whether an information society is a complete break from the past or merely a new label to describe the same type of society (Webster, 2006). Even though scholars have not agreed whether an information society is something new, this concept has been appropriated by international organizations such as the OCED, which promotes an information economy to be one of the future. Governments that fail to design policies to accommodate such an economy will fall behind. At the end of the story, only those who join prevail. However, I asked whether these countries are competing in an existing space marked by information or whether information actually creates a new sense of time and space.

This chapter then turned to the relationship between information, space, and time. I suggested that different types of information allow us to imagine new spaces, tying the past to the future in different ways. For example, the discovery of the double helix allows us to visualize the existence of DNA structure inside our body; genome mapping connects us to the past and helps us project the future. In another example, online databases ask us to see knowledge as boundless, freed from the constraints of printed materials stored in a physical location.

This book defines information in relation to space and time, all three concepts are fluid. Different types of information co-exist in different senses of time and space. Information can be analogue—such as that shared in a face-to-face conversation or that scribbled on a piece of paper—and digital (Floridi, 2010). Information can have a broad or narrow purpose; and it does not necessarily need to move society forward. For example, family recipes may only be shared among a handful of people, but it is valuable information to those who belong to the family. This subjective knowledge is valuable to those in the family even though it does not sell online advertising space and attract online buzz.

By expanding the definition of information to include analogue information and local knowledge and by seeing information as space and time interdependent, this definition stands a chance to include populations who are traditionally not seen as participants of an information society. These participants are not merely passive receivers of information, but they are active agents who shape time and space through producing, distributing, and consuming information. By using a broad definition, representations of information will then include hands of women, people of color, manual laborers, older people, and people with disabilities who use a wide range of technological tools to make information that is meaningful to them.

BIBLIOGRAPHY

Ancestry and traits service. (n/a). 23andMe. Retrieved from: https://www.23andme.com/dna-ancestry/?vip=true&pdp=true

Babe, R. E. (1995). *Communication and the transformation of economics: Essays in information, public policy, and political economy.* Boulder, CO: Westview Press.

Becker, J., & Hayes, R. M. (1963). *Information storage and retrieval: Tools, elements, theories*. New York: Wiley.

Bell, D. (1973). *The coming of post-industrial society: A venture in social forecasting*. New York: Basic Books.

Buckland, M. (2017). *Information and society*. Cambridge, MA: MIT Press.

Buckland, M., & Liu, Z. (1998). History of information science. In T. B. Hahn & M. Buckland (Eds.), *Historical studies in information society* (pp. 272–295). Medford, NJ: Information Today.

Bush, V. (1945, July). As we may think. *The Atlantic*. Retrieved from: https://www.theatlantic.com/magazine/archive/1945/07/as-we-may-think/303881/

Castells, M. (2004). An introduction to the information age. In F. Webster, R. Blom, E. Karvonen, H. Melin, K. Nordenstreng, & E. Puoskari (Eds.), *The information society reader* (pp. 138–149). London: Routledge.

Castells, M. (2010). *The information age: Economy, society and culture Volume 1: The rise of the network society* (2nd ed.). Oxford: Wiley Blackwell.

Center for the Mathematics of Information. (n/a). California Institute of Technology. Retrieved from: https://www.cmi.caltech.edu/

Chow-White, P. A. (2008). The informationalization of race: Communication technologies and the Human Genome in the digital age. *International Journal of Communication, 2*, 1168–1194.

Collins, F. S. (n/a a). Double helix. National Human Genome Research Institute. Retrieved from https://www.genome.gov/genetics-glossary/Double-Helix

Collins, F. S. (n/a b). Genome. National Human Genome Research Institute. Retrieved from https://www.genome.gov/genetics-glossary/Genome

Collman, A. (2018, September 21). Long-lost siblings have emotional reunion after 23andMe kit brought them together 34 years after they were abandoned in South Korea. *Insider*. Retrieved from: https://www.insider.com/dna-test-helps-reunite-long-lost-siblings-after-34-years-2018-9

Committee on Public Information. (1920). *Complete report of the Chairman of the Committee on Public Information*. Washington, DC: Government Printing Office.

Dronamraju, K. R. (1999, November 1). Erwin Schrödinger and the origins of molecular biology. *Genetics, 153*(3), 1071–1076.

Escobar, A. (1999). Gender, place and networks: A political economy of cyberculture. In W. Harcourt (Ed.), *Women@internet: Creating new cultures in cyberspace* (pp. 31–54). London: Zed.

Floridi, L. (2010). *Information: A very short introduction*. Oxford: Oxford University Press.

Friedman, T. (2005). *The world is flat: A brief history of the twenty-first century*. New York: Farrar, Straus and Giroux.

García-Sancho, M. (2006). The rise and fall of the idea of genetic information (1948–2006). *Genomics, Society, and Policy, 2*(3), 16–36.

Gleick, J. (2011). *The information: A history, a theory, a flood*. New York: Vintage.

Haraway, D. J. (1997). *Modest_witness@second_millennium_femaleMan©_meets_OncoMouse™: Feminism and technoscience*. New York: Routledge.

Hassan, R. (2008). *The information society*. Cambridge: Polity.

Herner, S. (1984). Brief history of information science. *Journal of the American Society for Information Science, 35*(3), 157–163.

Hong, E. (2016, August 26). 23andMe has a problem when it comes to ancestry reports for people of color. *Quartz*. Retrieved from: https://qz.com/765879/23andme-has-a-race-problem-when-it-comes-to-ancestry-reports-for-non-whites/

Information and communication technology (ICT). (n/a). OECD Library. Retrieved from: https://www.oecd-ilibrary.org/science-and-technology/information-and-communication-technology-ict/indicator-group/english_o4df17c2-en

Kay, L. E. (2000). *Who wrote the book of life? A history of the genetic code*. Stanford, CA: Stanford University Press.

Lang, L. (2014, May 27). Oprah Winfrey's surprising DNA test. *Ancestry*. Retrieved from: https://blogs.ancestry.com/cm/the-surprising-facts-oprah-winfrey-learned-about-her-dna/

Marcus, A. D. (2020, July 24). Insights found into Americans' African descent. *Wall Street Journal*, p. A5.

Mattelart, A., & Mattelart, M. (1998). *Theories of communication: A short introduction* (S. G. Taponier & J. A. Cohen trans.). London: Sage.

Moody, G. (2004). *Digital code of life: How bioinformatics is revolutionizing science, medicine, and business*. Hoboken, NJ: John Wiley.

Nelkin, D., & Lindee, M. S. (1995). *The DNA mystique: The gene as a cultural icon*. New York: W. H. Freeman.

OECD. (2017). *OECD Digital Economy Outlook 2017*. Paris: OECD Publishing.

OECD. (2019). *Measuring the digital transformation: A roadmap for the future*. Paris: OCED Publishing.

Parry, B. (2004). *Trading the genome: Investigating the commodification of bio-information*. New York: Columbia University. Press.

Petersen, R., Pan, L., & Blanck, H. M. (2019, April 11). Racial and ethnic disparities in adult obesity in the United States: CDC's tracking to inform state and local action, *16*. Retrieved from: https://www.cdc.gov/pcd/issues/2019/18_0579.htm

PhD in mathematics of information (CDT). (n/a). Graduate Admissions. University of Cambridge. Retrieved from: https://www.graduate.study.cam.ac.uk/courses/directory/mapmpdmal

Poynter, G., & de Miranda, A. (2000). Inequality, work and technology in the services sector. In S. Wyatt, F. Henwood, N. Miller, & P. Senker (Eds.), *Technology and in/equality: Questioning the information society* (pp. 172–196). New York: Routledge.

Pray, L. (2008). Discovery of DNA structure and function: Watson and Crick. *Nature Education, 1*(1), p. 100.

Reitz, J. M. (n/a). *Online dictionary for library and information science*. Santa Barbara, CA: ABC-CLIO.

Ritchie, D. (2004). Information as metaphor: Biology and communication. In S. Braman (Ed.), *Information as metaphor: Biology and communication* (pp. 39–61). Mahwah, NJ: Lawrence Erlbaum.

Saracevic, T. (1992). Information science: Origin, evolution and relations. In P. Vakkari & B. Cronin (Eds.), *Conceptions of library and information science: Historical, empirical and theoretical perspectives* (pp. 5–27). London: Routledge.

Schiller, D. (1988). How to think about information? In V. Mosco & J. Wasko (Eds.), *The political economy of information* (pp. 27–41). Madison, WI: University of Wisconsin Press.

Schönlieb, C.-B. (2017, March 20). Uncovering the mathematics of information. *Plus magazine*. Retrieved from: https://plus.maths.org/content/uncovering-mathematics-information

Science Advisory Committee. (1963). *Science, government, information*. Washington, DC: Government Printing Office.

Spencer, G. (2005, August 31). New genome comparison finds chimps, humans very similar at the DNA level. National Human Genome Research Institute. Retrieved from: https://www.genome.gov/15515096/2005-release-new-genome-comparison-finds-chimps-humans-very-similar-at-dna-level

Thacker, E. (2006). *The global genome: Biotechnology, politics, and culture*. Cambridge, MA: MIT Press.

von Baeyer, H. C. (2004). *Information: The new language of science*. Cambridge, MA: Harvard University Press.

Waldby, C. (2000). *Visible human project: Informatic bodies and posthuman medicine*. London: Routledge.

Webster, F. (2006). *Theories of information society* (3rd ed.). Abingdon, UK: Routledge.

"What is library and information science?" (n/a). Information School. University of Washington. Retrieved from: https://ischool.uw.edu/programs/mlis/what-is-library-science

Zaloom, C. (2003). Ambiguous numbers: Trading technologies and interpretation of financial markets. *American Ethnologist, 30*(2), 258–272.

3
SEARCHING

INTRODUCTION

Searching is a deliberate act of looking for something or someone. When we search with a purpose, we can reasonably expect that we will find what we are looking for. However, searching in an offline world may have a higher degree of uncertainty than that in an online world for there is not always a system of information organization and retrieval in an offline world. In an online world, information needs to be organized first before retrieving and searching take place.

Let's think about searching for love. In an offline world, it is hard to know exactly when and where the love object will appear. Traditional wisdom teaches us to go to more social gatherings or hit a bar. Yet being in such places does not guarantee one would meet others who are also yearning for love, less someone who might fit one's vision of an ideal lover. In contrast, searching for love online may be easier because there are websites that organize potential partners' information for searches. Users can choose services based on sexual preferences, age, or even education levels. Then they can search for people who share their lifestyles and hobbies. Even though these online match making sites do not guarantee success, they eliminate one big headache in dating, which is finding out information about potential lovers.

The above example shows that information organization and retrieval are necessary to make online match making easy. Because online searches appear to be easy, we often do not think about the social implications of information search and retrieval (Gillespie, 2010). It is as if that search engines were passively waiting for humans to use them. However, this book chapter argues that search practices have profound social implications. In particular, they constitute systems of information and knowledge.

One social implication is that whether there will still be common knowledge. The explosion of apps promises users with easy to reach, highly personalized information. Even though users can easily look up sports scores or daily weather or breaking news from online newspapers, customizable search engines and phone apps promise to deliver the most relevant information based on users' interests and search histories. If everyone only receives highly customized information, then will there still be shared knowledge and a common worldview in a society? Some have already worried that news feed tend to give users only stories with similar viewpoints. If we never read about alternative viewpoints, we may believe that our viewpoints are the only possible one. Highly customized information then leads to a highly polarized society in which everyone only believes in one viewpoint and disregards others. In this chapter, we aim to examine this and more social implications of information organization and retrieval by answering three central questions.

How Do Humans Organize Information?

Humans have always developed systems to organize information for search and retrieval. Before digital technologies, humans organized books in a library, telephone numbers in a directory, words in a dictionary, and knowledge in an encyclopedia. These systems also allowed for quick information retrieval. Although few of us may consult a hard copy of a dictionary or an encyclopedia now, these systems have influenced information organization and retrieval in an online world. For example, library still calls its search engine an online "catalogue" and the phone directory icon on the smartphone still looks like a phone book. What are some systems to organize information for search and retrieval in an offline world?

What Implications Does Information Organization Have on Information and Knowledge?

No information organization system is neutral, information organization and retrieval have implications on our worldview, including how we understand gender and race. We will examine three social implications of some information organization systems: the disembedding of knowledge from the knowers; a western bias of information organization; and the homogenizing of knowledge. All these make knowledge appear to be objective and value-free.

What Is Information Literacy?

Searching for online information is recognized as a learned skill. The online space is simultaneously seen as both a vast land of knowledge *and* a lawless Wild West. Online users are asked to be purposeful in online searches but vigilant about hidden dangers in the online world. For example, finding love online is often said to be dangerous; many stories news reported about scams that cost love-seekers a fortune. To empower users to purposefully serve for online information, associations of higher education and library have developed frameworks of teaching and learning information literacy. However these frameworks very often fail to take into account unbalanced power relations between users and companies that provide information.

HOW HUMANS ORGANIZE INFORMATION FOR RETRIEVAL

The phrase "to search" is now synonymous with "to look up information online". But some still prefer to look up information from prints, such as looking up a word in a hardback dictionary or locating a major highway on a road atlas. In fact, the way that dictionaries and road atlases organize information can sometimes save users' time because how information is organized has implications for how it is retrieved. In the following, I look at how different types of information is organized and retrieved before the digital age: library catalogue, encyclopedia, dictionary, train timetable, telephone book, and map. I will also look at how an early Internet portal organized webpages.

Library Catalogue

Library catalogue is a database that shows items owned by a library. In a digital age, we search for items by typing in a search term and specifying what type of information it is: keyword, title, author, subject, ISBN number, or call number. Our queries will return with a result: either the library has the item or not.

Before the library catalogue became electronic, it was housed in a cabinet with multiple card drawers, each held thousands of cards with handwritten or typed information of a catalogue item. On each of the cards, patrons can look up information about the author, title, publisher, call number, and subjects. If the patrons locate the materials that they need from the catalogue, then they can visit the stacks and look for the books. Patrons will find books of the same subject placed next to each other on the shelf so that you will discover more titles of the same subject matter.

Is subject matter the only way that books can be grouped together on the bookshelves? Can they be grouped according to authors or publishers or even colors? How books should be organized in a library was an interest of Charles Ammi Cutter, an American librarian whose ambition was to develop a classification system that is "comprehensive of all human knowledge yet serviceable to the general user" (Sheola, 2010). He designed the Cutter system for libraries of different sizes. For the smallest ones, he decided that eight classes of subject matters would suffice (works of reference and general works; philosophy and religion; biography; history and geography and travels; social sciences; natural sciences and art; language and literature; and fiction). For larger libraries, he believed that 35 classes would work better.

Despite the Cutter classification system was the first one in the U.S., the Library of Congress system was more widely adopted. The Library of Congress system built upon Cutter's vision and has 21 classes of subjects: it begins with general works, then philosophy, psychology, and religion. Each of the classes also has subclasses which further classify titles into niche areas.

Encyclopedia

An encyclopedia offers summaries of knowledge of a wide range of topics. In print form, an encyclopedia usually has multiple volumes. For example, the latest edition of *The new encyclopaedia Britannica* has 32 volumes. Each of them comprises of articles arranged in an alphabetical order. The first article in the first volume is the topic "accounting" and the last topic in the last volume is "zoroastrianism and parsiism".

Users can quickly retrieve the appropriate volume by looking at the spine of each volume which shows the letters of the first words of the article titles. They can quickly flip to the pages by looking at the top right-hand corner that indicates the topic. The information about each topic is organized in a similar manner. For example, the article about "information processing" in *Encyclopaedia Britannica* begins with a brief definition of information and an explanation why this term gained more currency in the 20th century. It then states the basic concepts of information and distinguishes information as a resource from a commodity (see Chapter 6, "Creating", about the distinction). The bulk of the article focuses on elements of information processing, such as acquisition and recording of analog and digital information; inventory, organization, retrieval, display, and dissemination of information. The entry concludes with a bibliography. This entry, like others, gives readers a short and concise guide to the topic, yet it does not offer competing theoretical frameworks. It is more interested in laying out "facts" than presenting a debate.

The print form of encyclopedia may appear to be obsolete in the digital age where users can easily search for any information online. Yet, when patrons have little idea about a topic, encyclopedia is very helpful at providing basic information. In addition, patrons can be assured that the articles are well-written and are penned by experts. *Encyclopaedia Britannica* highlights the reasons why it is still relevant in a digital age: the expert writers are proficient about the topics, the articles are readable and accurate because they were "fact-checked, edited, and copyedited" (see Chapter 5, "Using", about misinformation) ("Introduction", n/a). In addition, it relies on "star power" of renowned expert-contributors, such as Milton Friedman writing about money, James Gleick writing about physicist Richard Feynman. The quality of the information is used to justify the high price tag. Because of the perceived quality, print copies of encyclopedia may be purchased and displayed in upper-middle-class households to show the owners' thirst of knowledge and cultural capital.

The history of encyclopedia illustrates that this publication was not for the average readers, but the learned men. *Encyclopaedia Britannica* was first printed in late 1800s on a commission by "a society of gentlemen" who wanted to provide "accurate definitions and explanations" of terms ("First edition", n/a). Even in a digital age, the front page of *Encyclopaedia Britannica* aims to curate knowledge for learned users rather than serving as an all-purpose search engine. For example, on March 17, 2020, one-third of the page provides FAQs about COVID-19. On the rest of the page, it introduces *The scarlet letter*, its author Nathaniel Hawthorne, the theme of puritanism, and its place in American literature.

Dictionary

A dictionary standardizes the meanings, sounds, and usage of words in a language. For languages that are made up of the alphabet, words are organized from A to Z. Like an encyclopedia, users can quickly flip to the appropriate page on which the word they search for is located. Typological languages (such as Chinese) organize information in other ways (such as the number of strokes or the radicals for Chinese).

Even though the dictionary seems to be an essential tool, it was not until 1755 that Johnson's dictionary was published. The most authoritative dictionary of the English language, *The Oxford English Dictionary (OED)*, was only completed in 1928, 70 years after the project commenced. According to *The meaning of everything* (Winchester, 2004), James Murray was commissioned by the Oxford University Press to publish a four-volume dictionary that includes all English vocabulary. Murray and his team asked readers to send in clips from printed work that shows how words were used in context. Murray did not live to complete his work. He might not even have guessed that the ten-volume work would take another 39 years to complete.

The dictionary is a living book because language constantly evolves. Every four months, the *OED* announces new additions. These new words became "official" after their circulation among English speakers.

For example, *OED* added the phrase "man hug" in March 2020, even though the first occurrence took place decades ago in 1970s.

Train Timetable

Train passengers check the train schedule to ensure that they know when to catch the train to arrive at their destination on time. The earliest train timetables were simple because there were only a few scheduled rides. For example, the Liverpool and Manchester Railway issued a poster to announce the schedule of four first-class coaches and two second-class coaches from Monday to Saturday. The bulk of the poster, however, was about where to buy tickets and bus transportation between stations ("Liverpool and Manchester Railway", n/a). In the U.S. railway companies carried advertisements in local newspapers to announce the schedule, ticket fare, and where to buy tickets. Posters were also printed and displayed in stations, hotels, and other public places. Later on, railway companies also printed small cards to distribute to passengers ("A short history", n/a).

Few of us would ponder how the train schedule has standardized time. Before the railway, populations in different places observed different times. They told time from the sundial rather than a mechanical clock. However, the discrepancy in local times meant that trains would not arrive and depart at designated time and there was a danger that they would collide. To avoid such discrepancies, regional time was standardized. The question was then which regional time should be used as a standard. In England, it was obvious that the time in London would become the standard time. In the mid-19th century, the British railway adopted Greenwich Mean Time (GMT) as the standard, commonly called the Railway Time. Later, GMT became the official time in Great Britain ("How did railways", n/a).

In the United States, a standardized national time would not work because of its vast geographical area. The country then adopted five time zones (Eastern, Central, Mountain, Pacific, and Alaska) in 1918. Similar to Great Britain, the proliferation of railroads probed the Interstate Commerce Commission to standardize time ("History of times zones", n/a). The standardization of national time also brought the standardization of international time. In 1884, the world was divided into 24 time zones with GMT being the standard, for two reasons: first, the U.K. had already chosen GMT as the basis for its own national time zone system; second, the majority of sea traffic used Greenwich as the Prime Meridian (i.e. zero degrees longitude) ("History of time zones", n/a). All these cases of time standardization show that ground and sea transportation required accurate calculation of time and space so as to ensure vessel safety.

Telephone Directory

The telephone was once a luxury so its ownership symbolized wealth and testified one's class status. The first telephone book was a piece of cardboard with the names and addresses of the exclusive 50 telephone owners (Eschner, 2017). However, the earliest phone books had no phone numbers because the owners would call the switchboard operator who then connected the callers. The telephone directory was a descendent of a city directory which listed the name, profession, home and business addresses of who's who in the city. The city directory was a vanity because residents had to pay to get themselves listed (Sutton, 2010). The earliest telephone and city directories were then less about a comprehensive documentation of every resident in a place, but those who would like to advertise their wealth in an exclusive club.

When switching became automatic and no longer relied on the operators, phone directories listed phone numbers along with names and addresses (Nilsson, 2010). The telephone directories also branched out into white pages for households and yellow pages for businesses. When the telephone became less of a luxury and more of a household necessity, the telephone directory became a more reliable document of all the residents' names in a town or city. The information was organized by the alphabetical order of the owners' last names. Users can flip to the page quickly and identify the person. The yellow pages organized the information by businesses types (such as doctor, law firms, and so on). It therefore served as an important advertising platform for small businesses; they could pay more to have a large space to get more exposure.

Local telephone companies used to deliver the yellow and white pages to households and businesses for free. They were also available next to public telephones in bus terminals, train stations, and restaurants. With the popularity of mobile phones and the Internet, the telephone books became obsolete. Piles of deliveries were left outside buildings' front doors with no takers. However, users could continue requesting a printed copy to be delivered to their homes. Nowadays, telephone directory printers call the hard copy "the original search engine". Ironically, with the decline of landlines, the phones may once again become more exclusive because low-income families and younger people rely on their mobile phone numbers, only households with older adults who have the means to pay for landlines will have their information listed in the phone book.

Maps

Map is one of the oldest technologies that humans use to organize spatial information that helps navigate the surroundings. The oldest map known was created in 25,000 BC in what is now the Czech Republic (Czechia). This map was carved out of a mammoth tusk on which a hunting landscape was shown. Archeologists believed hunter-gatherers depicted their environment by using map ("Mammmoth tusk from Pavlov", n/a). Maps were later used by ancient civilizations for administration purposes; they documented world expedition, empire building, and city planning. While train time schedule standardized time, maps standardized space (Giddens, 1990).

In this section, I focus on Rand McNally, a name that is synonymous with the American highways. A copy of Rand McNally map instills in drivers a sense of security because it helps navigate the vast land. The popularity of a road map also shows the U.S. government effort to plan its highway system to connect the nation. The road map also symbolizes a rite of passage for American youths when they embark on summer road trips to criss-cross the country.

Rand McNally began their business in response to the railroad era by printing tickets and timetables for Chicago railroads and railway guide. Its first map for automobile was published for New York City. In the early 20th century, another map company invented the "page-and-grid" system that aids users to identify specific spots on the map more easily. This system divided a map into grids by marking columns with numbers and rows with letters. To find a specific street, users would flip to the back and look up the street names listed in alphabetical order. Once they see the column's number and the row's letter that follow the street number, they flip back to the map and look up that street in the specific box.

Also in the early 20th century, Rand McNally began to mark highway numbers on the state maps. During that time, trains were still the main transportation means from one state or region to another. Therefore, there was not much concerted national effort to number interstate highways (highways within states were however numbered). It was not until the mid-20th century when automobiles became more affordable was interstate highway system being constructed. The popularity of the Rand McNally roadmap not only reflected how maps help drivers navigate their surroundings, but they also reflected how a nation uses roads to connect different regions into one single country.

Online Directory

So far we have looked at systems that organize analogue information. Most of the information is now digitized and the systems to organize and retrieve vocabulary, knowledge, train schedules, telephone numbers, and cartographical information have also migrated online. The last information organization and retrieval system reviewed here attempted to organize digital information but it heavily borrowed from previous systems.

Yahoo! began as an online directory to categorize an explosive growth of webpages that could be accessed by the public. In the earliest day of the commercial Internet, users needed an URL address to access a webpage. The Internet was less a universe for exploration, more a depository where webpages could be loaded only if the users had the correct address. It was not unlike a library with no open stacks: users could go and ask for any title if they already know what they are looking for. If they did not have any exact title in mind, this library is not useful. What Yahoo! did was to organize webpages into a directory so that users can look up relevant information by subject matters. The earliest Yahoo! directory was like the library catalogue where books are catagorized into subject matters. The online directory was manually curated by Yahoo employees. Such an online directory had become impossible to maintain after a short period of time when the number of webpages increased exponentially. Yahoo! then refashioned itself into a search engine and a mail service, then an online portal. Its popularity sharply declined when newcomers such as AOL Online and Google challenged it in various markets.

All in One? The Births of the Giants

One difference between analogue systems of information organization and retrieval and today's digital systems is that one single company can monopolize the entire ecosystem. Smartphones are already loaded with apps that help organize vocabulary, knowledge, telephone numbers, train schedules, and cartographical information. This one-stop-shop promotes ease: users can look up knowledge from Wikipedia and switch to a live bus schedule in a fraction of a second. In addition, how we look up one kind of information is like how we look up another kind of information. The search box has become ubiquitous whether we want to type in a difficult word or our location. If all information is collapsed into the same thing, then what are some impacts of search on human knowledge? This is the question we will explore in the next section.

THE SOCIAL IMPLICATIONS OF INFORMATION ORGANIZATION AND RETRIEVAL

I discuss in this section three social implications of how information organization and retrieval for our understanding of knowledge. I will continue drawing on the previous examples—library catalogue, encyclopedia, dictionary, train timetable, telephone directory, and map—for the discussion. I highlight that information organization and retrieval systems have a long-lasting impact on human understanding of knowledge (Hillis, Petit, & Jarnett, 2013). Contrary to some beliefs, digital technologies have not brought complete disruptions to analogue information systems and changed how humans understand knowledge. In this section, I will focus on three social implications found in both analogue and digital information organizations: (1) the disembedding of knowledge from the knowers; (2) the western bias of information organization; and (3) the homogenization of knowledge.

The Disembedding of Knowledge from the Knowers

Organizing information very often relies on disembedding knowledge from the knowers (Borgmann, 1999; Giddens, 1990). This process makes information an external "thing" that appears to be neutral. Knowledge is then seen to be free of bias from the subjects who produce it. This process standardizes information by eliminating local varieties, making only some information the formal and correct version (Eisenstein, 1979).

Map is a good illustration to show how this disembedding process works. Humans' understanding of space is always an embodied experience. We move in a space to know where we are and where we are heading. This experience is also highly individualized because our bodies respond to the environment differently. For example, for the able-bodied populations, we can walk up stairs in a building. Those in a wheelchair or with a baby stroller have to find an elevator to visit other floors.

Maps disembed knowledge from the knowers because they aid humans understand space even if we don't move in one. We can consult a map that represents space on a two-dimensional plane and plan how we move from point A to point B. Google Maps also offers street-level images for us to visualize navigation in a three-dimensional space.

While maps have objectively shown how space is organized, they also ask humans to use specific ways to experience space. To give an example, a roadmap points out which highways drivers should take to reach their destination. But the roadmap does not inform drivers their embodied experience such as the smell of trees and the sounds of traffic. In contrast, wild animals that live close to the highways pick up smell and sound to know where they should go and where they should avoid. Maps disembed knowledge from the knowers because they make a bodily experience less important while highlighting information such as geographical location.

Another example of knowledge being disembedded from knowers is printing technology. Before printing, knowledge was mostly localized and oral-based. Knowledge of subject matters and word meanings were contextualized in daily activities and communal experience. For example, linguists have shown that the Inuit populations have a wide range of words that mean snow (Robson, 2013). Their rich vocabulary of snow shows localized knowledge that is essential to day-to-day survival. However, when their territories were forced to be incorporated into countries such as the U.S. and Canada, the official language of English fails to capture the rich language about snow. The declining number of Inuit speakers may further threaten a historical and localized understanding about snow.

The Western Bias of Information and Its Organization

I have shown that information systems disembed knowledge from the knowers, resulting in information appearing to be a bias-free collective intelligence. However, what is often obscured is who decides what information is useful and what is not. This in turn obscures power relations between the ones who organize information and the users of the information systems.

Library systems are by no means unbiased, they privilege western knowledge as well as Judeo-Christian religious beliefs. For example, the catalogue of the Library of Congress has the subclass "Religions. Mythology. Rationalism". Under 660–2680 "History and principles of religions", it begins with European/Occidental (Classical, Germanic and Norse, other European) then Asian/Oriental and African. This order shows that the history of religions that came from Europe has priority than those that came from Asia and Africa. Another bias is shown through the assumed complexity and completeness of knowledge. For example, under Class D "World History and history of Europe", there are 16 subclasses about British and European countries but only one each about Asia, Africa, and Oceania. The drastic difference in the number of subclass may imply that knowledge about European histories are more specialized while that about Asia, Africa, and Oceania is general enough to be lumped into one subclass. Both the ordering and the number of subclasses show that knowledge about Europe is more profound and expansive than that about Asia, the Middle East, and Africa even though ancient civilizations are rooted in those regions.

In addition to library classification systems, maps and train timetables also illustrate western bias. Hodgkinson (1991) documented the

Eurocentrism of the world map. Our eyes tend to look at the centre and upper part of an image before moving down to the bottom and the periphery. Most of the world's maps show Europe in the centre of the map. In addition, it has pointed out that most world maps increase the size of Europe while decreasing that of Africa (Georgiou, 2018). To counter the western bias of world maps, some maps re-orient continents' positions to offer an alternative version of the world. For example, some put Greenland in the centre; others put Asia and Africa in the upper half. By re-configuring the positions, Europe is still at the centre but its size has significantly shrunk; the North American continent looks smaller and occupies as much space as the South American continent.

Time zones on the world map also reflect the hegemony of European colonialism over the rest of the world. Even till these days, the time of Western Europe is the norm; the Coordinated Universal Time (formerly known as Greenwich Mean Time) is the time of Great Britain. Located in Greenwich is the Prime Meridian that marks the zero longitude which divides the hemisphere into West and East. Unlike the northern and southern hemisphere which is divided by the equator (which is determined by the axis of earth's rotation), the location of the Prime Meridian is completely arbitrary. Countries used to draw up their prime meridians until Greenwich Meridian was elected to be the international standard by delegates from a mere 25 countries.

The importance of Greenwich Meridian is more than its symbolic value. It also documents the British Empire's maritime superiority which was essential to seizing foreign lands as colonies and trading ports. The Royal Observatory that is located in Greenwich has a museum to document the British Empire's accomplishments in timekeeping technologies. Most appropriately, the National Maritime Museum, next to the Royal Observatory, also records naval history.

Homogenization of Knowledge

I have so far explained two social implications of information systems: disembedding knowledge from the knowers; and western bias in information standardization. In this section, I suggest that both processes homogenize knowledge by eroding local varieties, deeming them less legitimate than the official version (Borgmann, 1999; Segev, 2010).

Dictionary standardizes vocabulary. Words in the *Oxford English Dictionary* (*OED*) represent standard usage. The *OED* explains that "standard English" is "generally appropriate in most situations and contexts. It is typically the language of official communication, broadcasting, and printed matter" (*OED*, 2004, p. 1696). Those that are deemed less than standard are marked with *alt.* (alteration), *colloq.* (colloquial), *dial* (dialect), *pop.* (popular), *sl.* (slang), and *var* (variant). The *OED* also denotes the origins of some words, such as *Amer.* as American English or *Canad.* as Canadian. It however acknowledges that standard English is not equivalent to correct or superior English, but one that is the most *official* to communicate with a wider public. This definition makes local varieties less official and are meant to be for a narrower audience.

As suggested, the train timetable eroded local time. Trains bridged distances and connected remote places. Before the train was the main transportation mode, travel between places would take hours if not days. Prior to trains, discrepancies of local times did not affect travel that much because travel time was imprecise and hard to estimate. However, when train became a popular transportation mode, it was possible to estimate travel time making it predictable. Because time could be quantified, discrepancies in local times then could make railway travel tricky or even dangerous. For example, in Britain, local times used to have a 20-minute difference. If the passengers did not change their watches throughout the journey, they would arrive the destination 20 minutes earlier or later than the timetable that was set in local time. Moreover, if different trains ran on local times, then there was a chance of collision. Time standardization is necessary for safety but it also eliminates local time, told by the sun.

In a more extreme example, even though China spans five time zones, the country's leaders believed that five different time zones would fragment the nation. Therefore, the country adopted one time zone. This standardized time makes it difficult for local populations to carry out their daily lives because when residents in the most eastern part begin their day, those in the western part are still in the middle of the night.

The homogenization of information is also apparent in the digital age. Even though many have argued that the Internet has allowed users freedom because the sources are more diverse, it is also true that information retrieval has homogenized our experience of information. In the analogue era, we consulted specific information sources for specific information, such as the dictionary for words and road map for driving locations. In the digital age, we search for information in almost the same way: by typing keywords in the search bar. For example, when I type in any word in my computer's search box, the results tell me all the files and folders in my computer that have the specific word. In addition, they search for online news articles that have the specific word. While the all-in-one search is convenient, the search result presentation gives an illusion that all types of documents and results are of the same nature. In other words, a document that is written by me holds the same level of relevance and significance as an online news article.

Online search engines also create the same problem when it treats information of different nature to be of the same importance and relevance. For example, when I typed in the search term "searching constitution" to look up the Fourth Amendment of the U.S. Constitution, the result yielded webpages from a few reputable sources (such as Cornell Law School and the Library of Congress Library). Yet it also yielded irrelevant image files such as word search games. Obviously, word search games do not inform me the specific text from the Fourth Amendment, but when these irrelevant images are seen as parallel to an important text that guarantees people's rights, all the results appear to have the same importance and relevance. The illusion that every piece of information is as relevant and important as others lead some to call for the teaching and learning of information literacy. Like how educated people learn to read and write, educated online users should also learn how best to search for information. In the next section, I focus on the information literacy movement.

TEACHING AND LEARNING TO SEARCH

Searching online is an easy task; it only requires typing in a keyword in the search box. However, some training is required to learn how to choose specialized databases, use appropriate search terms, evaluate search results, use online information, as well as properly cite them. These skills are usually taught as part of an information literacy curriculum offered by librarians. Therefore, in this section, I will review how three organizations—the Association of American Colleges and Universities (AAC&U) and the American Library Association (ALA)—define and assess information literary. I conclude by asking if the teaching and learning of information literacy address the previously mentioned concerns: disembedding knowledge from the knowers; having a western bias; and homogenizing knowledge.

The Association of American Colleges and Universities (AAC&U) has 1,400 higher education institutions members. Its goal is to "[advance] the vitality and public standing of liberal education by making quality and equity the foundations for excellence in undergraduate education in service to democracy" ("About AAC&U", n/a). Information literacy, a skill that AAC&U stresses, can then be seen as an important skill to practice democracy.

The AAC&U defines information literacy as: "the ability to know when there is a need for information, to be able to identify, locate, evaluate, and effectively and responsibly use and share that information for the problem at hand" ("Information literacy VALUE rubric", n/a) Accordingly, the five criteria to assess whether college students are information-literate are the ability to:

(1) determine the extent of information needed;
(2) access the needed information;
(3) evaluate information and its sources critically;
(4) use information effectively to accomplish a specific purpose; and
(5) access and use information ethnically and legally.

(Rhodes, 2010)

At the highest level, a college-educated person is expected to:

- define the problem at hand, determine key concepts, find out the types of information that address to concepts or solve the problem;
- access information with effective and well-designed strategies;
- systematically analyze assumptions and evaluate the contexts when presenting a position;
- communicate, organize, and synthesize information from various sources;
- do correct citations, avoid plagiarism, and observe ethical use of information.

In contrast, a college-educated person demonstrates minimal information literacy skills when they randomly access information, retrieve irrelevant or poor-quality information, and present fragmented or misappropriated information.

To AAC&U, information literacy is not only limited to online information because college students are also expected to access and use a repertoire of information sources from prints—such as books and newspapers—to moving images and sounds—such as films and podcast; from old materials—such as archival materials and historical documents—to current ones—such as current news stories. The ability to differentiate different types of information and to understand the contexts under which such information was produced is a learned skill. On the other hand, if a college-educated person could only use a limited number of search strategies (such as an over-reliance on commercial search engines) or fail to contextualize the search results, then this person may have limited information literacy.

The AAC&U definition of information literacy does not overtly point out the disembedding of knowledge, the western bias and homogenization of information. In fact, their definition seems to imply that the *systems* for information organization are mostly value-free so students do not need to evaluate them. Students are only asked to evaluate whether the information, but not so much the systems. To give an example, a student may understand that the online databases of the Library of Congress (LoC) are reliable and this student may use it as an appropriate online database. Yet, this student will have little understanding how the design and interface of LoC databases may influence how they conduct information search. Therefore, AAC&U's definition does not take into account how the technologies of information organization enable and constrain information retrieval because they are embedded with specific values. Therefore, the definition of information literacy may need to include a critical understanding of the relationship between the technologies of information organization and the nature of knowledge.

When compared to AAC&U, the American Library Association (ALA) has a relatively critical stance towards information organization systems. ALA is a professional association for librarians in the U.S. ALA has a very similar definition of information literacy as AAC&U. They define it as an individual's ability to "recognize when information is needed and have the ability to locate, evaluate and use effectively the needed information" (American Library Association, 1989). The organization believes that information literacy plays an important role in developing individuals as informed citizens and community members, fostering lifelong learning, and having greater control over their own learning. It also shares a similar set of criteria of information literacy. It is notable that ALA does point out that information literacy involves understanding economic, legal, and social ramifications of information (American Library Association, 2000).

Unlike the AAC&U, ALA is more explicit about the relationship between information technology and information literacy. It differentiates "information literacy" from "fluency with technology": the former focuses on the "content, communication, analysis, information searching, and evaluation" and the latter "a deep understanding of technology and graduated, increasingly skilled use of it" (American Library Association, 2000, p. 3). While ALA acknowledges that technology fluency matters to information literacy, it believes that critical thinking is the utmost skill to attain such literacy. However, somewhat curiously, ALA suggests that technology use is independent of information literacy. This may imply that the nature of technologies has little to do with the information that it produces. In other words, information documented on a handwritten note may be the same as that in an email. In addition, like AAC&U, ALA does not see information organizations—such as library catalogue—as a form of technology which infrastructure needs to be critiqued.

Next I turn to the Association of College and Research Libraries (ACRL) to see how they define information literacy. When compared to AAC&U and its parent organization ALA, ACRL seems to have the most critical stance about power and information. ACRL issued an information literacy framework for higher education in 2016 (Association of College and Research Libraries, 2016). The aim of this framework is to help students, instructors, and librarians to navigate better the fast-changing higher education environment and the dynamic but uncertain information ecosystem. Two of the frames that I will focus on are "authority is constructed and contextual" and "information has value". These two frames may speak to the concerns of information organization and retrieval disembedding knowledge from the knowers, having a western bias, and homogenizing knowledge.

For the first frame "authority is constructed and contextual", ACRL suggested that information reflects creators' expertise and credibility and that different communities may recognize different types of authority. ACRL believes that an educated person should be able to recognize how authority may influence society. In addition, this person should be able to evaluate the bias and privileged embedded in information that is produced with authority. ACRL acknowledged that information is not neutral, the creators' worldviews, genders, sexual orientations, and cultural orientations could influence how they produce information.

For the second frame "information has value", ACRL recognizes that information has economic, social, political, and cultural values and that legal and socioeconomic interests would influence how and what information is produced and distributed. It further suggested that "the value of information is manifested in various contexts, including publishing practices, access to information, the commodification of information, and intellectual property laws" (Association of College and Research Libraries, 2016, p. 16). To them, an educated person is able to understand all these practices marginalize certain voices; but this understanding will also effect social, economic, civic, and personal changes. Searching is just a basic step, an educated person will also challenge these practices at appropriates times. Although ACRL does not specifically mention knowledge is disembedded from the knowers, the western bias and homogenization of knowledge, it is more critical than AAC&U and its parent organization ALA about the assumed neutrality of information systems.

CONCLUSION

I suggest in this chapter that searching online is a dual process of information organization and retrieval. Humans have always organized information so that we can locate relevant information quickly and effectively. For example, words are organized in a dictionary, knowledge is organized in an encyclopedia. However, these systems are not neutral, they are always laden with values. In this chapter, we examined three social implications of information organization: the disembedding of knowledge from knowers, the western bias of knowledge, and the homogenization of knowledge. Even though some have suggested that online searches are democratic because they allow users to access a large volume of diverse information, this chapter also warns that online search results conflate every piece of information to the same degree of relevance and importance.

Because of the vast amount of information, information literacy is argued to be a skill that an educated person should have in order to assess searched information and to use it in a context-relevant and critical manner. However, current definitions of information literacy fall short on illustrating how power works through designing information systems that impact human knowledge. In addition, the definitions of information literacy tend not to complicate the relationship between information and the technologies that organize and retrieve it. In Chapter 5, "Using", I will further show how organizations could use information to constrain individuals' freedom. Because of this, a non-critical definition of information literacy is not sufficient to illustrate how power works through the organization of information.

BIBLIOGRAPHY

About AAC&U. (n/a). *The Association of American Colleges and Universities.* https://www.aacu.org/about

American Library Association. (1989). *Presidential committee on information literacy: Final report.* Chicago: American Library Association. Retrieved from: http://www.ala.org/acrl/publications/ whitepapers/presidential

American Library Association. (2000). *Information literacy competency standards for higher education.* Chicago: American Library Association. Retrieved from: https://alair.ala.org/bitstream/handle/11213/7668/ACRL%20Information%20Literacy%20Competency%20Standards%20for%20Higher%20Education.pdf?sequence=1&isAllowed=y

Association of College and Research Libraries. (2016). *Framework for information literacy for higher education.* Chicago: The Association of College and Research Libraries. Retrieved from: http://www.ala.org/acrl/files/issues/infolit/framework.pdf

Borgmann, A. (1999). *Holding on to reality: The nature of information at the turn of the millennium.* Chicago: University of Chicago Press.

Eisenstein, E. L. (1979). *The printing press as an agent of change: Communications and cultural transformations in early-modern Europe (Vol I & II).* Cambridge, MA: Cambridge University Press.

Eschner, K. (2017, February 21). The first telephone book had fifty listings and no numbers. *Smithsonian Magazine.* Retrieved from: https://www.smithsonianmag.com/smart-news/first-telephone-book-had-fifty-listings-and-no-numbers-180962173/

First edition. (n/a). *Encyclopaedia Britannica*. Retrieved from: https://www.britannica.com/topic/Encyclopaedia-Britannica-English-language-reference-work

Georgiou, A. (2018, October 23). True scale map of the world shows how big countries really are. *Newsweek*. Retrieved from: https://www.newsweek.com/true-scale-map-world-shows-how-big-countries-really-are-1183386

Giddens, A. (1990). *The consequence of modernity*. Stanford, CA: Stanford University Press.

Gillespie, T. (2010). The politics of "platforms". *New Media and Society, 12*(3), 347–364.

Hillis, K., Petit, M., & Jarnett, K. (2013). *Google and the culture of search*. New York: Routledge.

History of time zones. (n/a). *Bureau of Transportation Statistics*. Retrieved from: https://www.bts.gov/geography/geospatial-portal/history-time-zones

Hodgkinson, K. (1991). Standing the world on its head: A review of eurocentrism in humanities maps and atlases. *Teaching History, 62*, 19–23.

How did railways lead to GMT becoming the UK time standard? (n/a). *Royal Museums Greenwich*. Retrieved from: https://www.rmg.co.uk/

Information literacy VALUE rubric. (n/a). *The Association of American Colleges and Universities*. Retrieved from: https://www.aacu.org/value/rubrics/information-literacy

Introduction. (n/a). *Encyclopaedia Britannica*. Retrieved from: https://www.britannica.com/topic/Encyclopaedia-Britannica-English-language-reference-work

Liverpool and Manchester Railway passenger timetable. (n/a). *Edge Hill*. Retrieved from: http://www.edgehillstation.co.uk/resources/liverpool-and-manchester-railway-passenger-timetable/

Mammoth tusk from Pavlov-The oldest Moravian map? (n/a). *Archaeological Institute of America*. Retrieved from: https://www.archaeological.org/event/mammoth-tusk-from-pavlov-the-oldest-moravian-map/

Nilsson, J. (2010, February 20). The book of numbers: A history of the telephone book. *The Saturday Evening Post*. Retrieved from: https://www.saturdayeveningpost.com/2010/02/book-numbers/

Oxford English Dictionary. (2004). (11th ed.). Oxford: Oxford University Press.

Rhodes, T. (2010). *Assessing outcomes and improving achievement: Tips and tools for using rubrics*. Washington, DC: Association of American Colleges and Universities.

Robson, D. (2013, January 14). There really are 50 Eskimo words for "snow". *The Washington Post*. Retrieved from: https://www.washingtonpost.com/national/health-science/there-really-are-50-eskimo-words-for-snow/2013/01/14/e0e3f4e0-59a0-11e2-beee-6e38f5215402_story.html

Segev, E. (2010). *Google and the digital divide: The bias of online knowledge*. Oxford: Chandes.

Sheola, N. (2010, June). Charles Ammi Cutter. *Boston Athenaeum*. Retrieved from: https://www.bostonathenaeum.org/library/book-recommendations/athenaeum-authors/charles-ammi-cutter

A short history of American Railway timetables. (n/a). *National Association of Timetable Collectors.* http://www.naotc.org/history/tt-history.htm#_Inception_to_Civil

Sutton, P. (2010, December 14). A look at "the book": The fall and rise of the telephone directory. New York Public library. Retrieved from: https://www.nypl.org/blog/2010/12/14/look-book-city-directory

Winchester, S. (2004). *The meaning of everything: The story of the Oxford English dictionary.* Oxford: Oxford University Press.

4

ACCESSING

INTRODUCTION

When Barack Obama was running for president in 2008, there was a conspiracy that he was not born in the U.S. and therefore ineligible to be the President. Despite the fact that this claim had no ground, he released his birth certificate during the campaign to prove that he is indeed a natural-born U.S. citizen. However, after the release of the electronic short-form birth certificate, the doubters were still not convinced that it proved anything. Some even claimed that it was a forgery because Obama chose not to release the original copy with signatures. In 2011, President Obama requested the Hawaii Department of Health to release a copy of the long-form birth certificate. A copy was posted on the White House website and has not been removed since he left office. When the controversy of Obama's birthplace happens again, the public is likely to further scrutinize the authenticity of this copy.

This controversy is one of many cases that ask us to reflect on *who* has the power to access whose information. Unequal power relations both reflect and are resulted from unequal information access. Therefore, this controversy is not about whether the public should have access to certain information. This controversy is about how power relations structure information access. In this case of Obama, racial relations in the U.S. have shaped who can ask for whom for certain information, even if the information is deemed private and confidential. Because President Obama self-identifies as a black man, his privacy may be less valued because of the legacy of slavery in the country. Slaves were the private property of owners; as such, they could not claim privacy to their lives. This unequal racial relation is illustrated in the Obama case when some felt they have the right to ask the black populations to prove their citizenship. The Obama birth certificate case therefore raises a few questions that this chapter aims to answer.

How Does an Interpretation of Information Mutually Constitute an Interpretation of Technology?

Doubters of Obama's short-form birth certificate believed that the electronic copy was a forgery. They believed that the original, long-form certificate would reveal whether the president was a natural-born U.S. citizen or not. Why are digital copies believed to be easily forged while handwritten or typed copies are believed to be more authentic? This case seems to imply that the *real* identity of the President lies on a piece of paper stored in Hawaii, not embedded by the pixels in a digital copy. The different interpretations of information show that it is not monolithic, it has different qualities through technological production, distribution, and consumption. Because of the mutually constitutive relationship between information and technology, those who control technologies could also control the interpretation of information.

Who Governs Information Access and How?

The media had repeatedly approached the Hawaii Department of Health to release a copy of Obama's long-form birth certificate. The department had refused to do so because state law prohibits persons who don't have "tangible interest" in the vital record from gaining access to the birth certificate. Even the personal counsel of the President had to be authorized by the President to request the release. How did an organization decide who have access to information?

How Is Information Access Related to Public Interest?

Information access is often tied to public interest. This is particularly the case during presidential election campaigns: candidates are asked to disclose information for the public to judge their moral characters. Would access to public figures' information serve public interest? The director of the Hawaiian Health Department did not think so (Fuddy, 2011). In addition, President Obama believed that "the distraction over [the] birth certificate wasn't good for the country. [...] it was bad for the American people and distracting from the many challenges we face as a country" (Pfeiffer, 2011, para. 3).Under what circumstances information access is a disservice to citizens?

Is the Public a Racialized Concept?

When doubters suggested that access to Obama's birth certificate is for public interest (Smith & Tau, 2011), who are the public in their mind? Are the public the indecisive registered voters who wished to know more about the candidates? Or are they white supremacists who believe the white race should dominate non-white races? The Obama birth certificate case shows that the name "public interest" was used as an excuse to disguise doubters' racism. The doubters may believe the public is an imagined group of white supremacists and the online space is where they could seek out each other (Daniels, 2009). In either case, doubters believe they have the right to ask for a piece of private document from a non-white candidate. Non-white voters, on the contrary, may not feel they have the power to ask white candidates to prove their natural-born citizenship status. In fact, if they do so, the election campaigns and the media may dismiss this request as unnecessary.

In the following, I will show there are many instances about information access that raise questions about who the public is. These instances happen in the U.S. as well as in other countries. In addition, these instances took place in recent time and in the distant past. In the following, I will first examine the mutually constitutive relationship between information and technologies.

HOW ARE INTERPRETATIONS OF INFORMATION AND TECHNOLOGIES MUTUALLY CONSTITUTIVE?

Information access, at the very basic, involves someone providing information for others. Both parties need the appropriate technologies to achieve the tasks. For example, the Obama campaign had to first upload a digital copy on the Internet, then users would need an Internet-connected device to view this file. However, information access also applies to analogue information. For example, the Hawaii Health Department store paper copies of birth certificates. State employees retrieve these copies for those who request a copy of their birth certificates.

Because different technologies are involved in storing and retrieving information, users would interpret the information differently even if the content is exactly the same. For example, retrieving the digital copy of Obama's certificate is easy. It only involves a simple search on the Internet. However, retrieving the original copy is very difficult. First, it is only released to the rightful owners or their representatives; second, ones would need to travel to a specific place in in Hawaii. This process is time-consuming and costly. However, if the original birth certificate would one day be accessible for public viewing in a museum in Hawaii, many will be willing to spend the time and money to view it even if they could look at it on the Internet at any time in any place. The desire to look at the original copy reflects a belief that it has a quality that is different from a digital copy, therefore it deserves a special trip to be viewed. In a similar way, art lovers travel long distance to look at original artwork; film buffs attend screenings to celebrate restored film reels.

What do the above tell us about the *quality* of information in digital and analogue eras? I argue in this section that information is not independent of the technology with and through which it is produced, distributed, and consumed. In other words, analogue technology (such as a typewriter) produces information of a different quality from digital technology (such as a computer). Accordingly, our understanding of information depends on our interpretation of the technology which produces the information. In this sense, information access is not simply about the availability of technology and information, but how the understanding of information frames that of technology and vice versa. When we take into account the interdependence between technology and information, we will understand that those who control technology can also control the meanings of information. If the ultimate goal of information accessibility is to ensure an open, transparent, and democratic sharing of information, then merely providing access is not enough. Openness, transparency, and democracy also depend on who designs and controls the technology and how they constrain the interpretation of information.

To illustrate the relationship between information and technology, I will first argue how two influential models of communication— Shannon and Weaver's transmission model and Marshall McLuhan's "hot/cool" media—give little consideration to the interdependent relationship between technology and information. Then I will discuss how two other models—Stuart Hall's encoding/decoding model and Walter Ong's literacy/orality—discussed this relationship. Among them, only Hall's model pays sufficient attention to how power shapes an understanding of information.

From the Transmission Model of Communication to "Hot/Cool" Media

One of the most influential models to explain the process of communication is Shannon and Weaver's transmission model of communication (see also Ch. 2 "defining" and a mathematical model of communication). In this model, a sender initiates a communication process by sending a message through a channel to a receiver. For example, I (*sender*) pick up the phone (*channel*) to call a friend (*receiver*) to invite that person to a party (*message*). Even though the primary concern of Shannon and Weaver was how the telephone could transmit signals with maximum efficiency, their model was adopted to understand all forms of human communication, including face to face interaction and mass communication. The adoption of this model to human communication has been vehemently critiqued (see Fiske, 1982) because it does not consider the motivations of communication and the interpretation of messages.

For the purpose here, I add that another flaw of this model is its inattention to the interdependence between information and technology.

The transmission model views technology being independent of information that is produced, distributed, and consumed by and through technology (Von Baeyer, 2004). As stated, the primary concern of Shannon and Weaver was an efficient transmission of communication signals. However, sometimes we may appreciate "flawed" communication signals over efficiency. For example, in the old days when signals of international calls were transmitted through copper wires, there were often delays, the sound quality was poor, and disruptions were frequent. Digital technology had drastically improved efficiency. When signals are transmitted through fibre optics, it is often hard to tell if one is talking to a person a few towns away or on the other side of the earth. However, some callers may miss the nostalgic feeling of listening to a voice that came from a land afar. The affect and emotions associated with poor sound quality transmitted by copper wires show that we interpret information in relation to technology. Similarly, we attach more emotions to a handwritten note and a typed letter than an email.

Another model that does not take into account the interdependent relationship between information and technology is that of Marshall McLuhan's "hot/cool" media. In fact, McLuhan had little regard for information. In *Understanding media* (1994), McLuhan suggested that too much attention has been paid to the effects that media messages have on the audience and too little on how the medium affects the audience. He believed that the medium—such as television, film, newspaper—shaped human communication. He differentiated hot media from cold media based on traits such as information richness, audience participation, and sensory stimulation. Hot media included photograph, radio, print, film, and books; cold media included cartoon, telephone, speech, television, and comics. Hot media privileges one sensory stimulation over others; such as the visual sense for photograph and print, the aural sense for radio. These media do not demand the audience to fill in much background information, and thus require little audience participation. At the same time, hot media require the audience to pay undivided attention because they are more stimulating. On the other hand, cold media such as comics and the telephone have less information; they demand the audience to fill in many more details, and thus require a higher level of audience participation. At the same time, they are less stimulating so the audience can easily be distracted from this medium to another. Advanced technologies have probably made some media "hotter" or "colder" than they were in 1960s when McLuhan first offered his theories. For example, high-definition television sets and high-quality television shows may make television as "hot" a medium as movies because they produce stimulating sounds and sights. The smartphone that combines multiple media (music player, telephone, television, and so on) may also make telephone a hot medium.

Similar to the transmission model of communication, McLuhan believed that technology is independent of the information that it distributes. I disagree with his assumption and assert that the information that is distributed through technologies matters to audience's participation as well. For example, even though the audience is required to pay undivided attention in a movie theater because of the dimmed environment, wide screen, and surround sound, the film genre also matters to the audience. If audience members do not care about the topic, they may not pay complete attention to this hot media. Similarly, we may not pay attention to telemarketers' calls but will give full attention to doctors' calls.

After reviewing two models that assume the independent relationship between information and technologies, I review two more models—Stuart Hall's "encoding/decoding" (1992) model and Walter Ong's orality/literacy—that have considered this interdependent relationship. Stuart Hall proposed an encoding/decoding model in which he privileged the *discursive* form of the message. He argued that any message must be packaged in a specific audiovisual form that is suitable for the technology through which it is transmitted. For example, a news event only becomes a news story when newsmakers recognize the significance of the event and are capable of telling the story. Moreover, a news story also requires news stations to have appropriate technical facilities. On the reception end, the audience also needs to understand why certain events are deemed newsworthy, why news stories are packaged in a certain format, and use appropriate technologies to consume the news stories.

Hall's model pays more attention to the interdependent relationship between technology and information. It is also applicable to how the audience understands information in a multi-screen era. For example, a news story watched on television is interpreted to be more reliable than the same one watched on YouTube. Even though news stories can be watched on different platforms on different devices, the audience still harbors a belief that those on television are the most reliable because newsmakers are believed to be professionals who carefully select the most salient news to broadcast during prime time (Robertson, 2007). In contrast, the audience tend to be more skeptical of the truthfulness of news that they watch on YouTube (Evans, 2016).

Another theorist whose work hinted at the mutually constitutive relationship between technologies and information was Walter Ong (2002). Ong was interested in how writing and printing technology changed humans' cognition and how it externalized human thoughts as information. From Ong's point of view, the transmission model of communication could only explain a writing culture because this model assumes information can be separated from the origin of the message. Because Ong believed that the message cannot exist independently of the speaker in an oral culture, his ideas can be used to critique the transmission model in a few ways. For example, the transmission fails to see the speaker being able to anticipate the response from the audience. According to Ong, the relationship between the speakers and the audience in an oral culture is intersubjective. This intersubjectivity helps communities formed through communication.

To further explain Ong's point, we need to review what he achieved in the magnum opus *Orality and literacy* (Ong, 2002). Ong opened the book by suggesting that those who grew up in primarily oral cultures organize thoughts and manage knowledge differently from those who grew up in writing-oriented cultures. The catalyst for the change from orality to literacy was the technology of writing. Writing instruments that enabled humans write down thoughts changed human consciousness and a sense of what is meant to be human. In an oral culture, one's thought ceases to exist when one passes away. In contrast, a writer's book will continue to be read even after the writer deceases. The technology of writing has thus separated the written words from the origins of the words (see Chapter 3, "Searching", about knowledge disembedded from the knower).

Ong continued to argue that the invention of printing has further enhanced the effects of writing on thought and expression. One effect of printing technology was the erosion of auditory processing, making humans more aware of the visual space because prints take up space. In contrast, social beings in an oral culture do not visualize space beyond the one that they are currently at because humans have to be in the same space at the same time to see and hear each other. Therefore, in an oral culture, the speakers and the audience engage in a performance through speech.

In comparison to the Shannon and Weaver's transmission model and McLuhan's hot and cold media, Hall's encoding-decoding model and Ong's orality/literacy paid attention to the interdependency between technology and information. They have both pointed out that neither information—as in the transmission model—nor technology—as in hot/cold media—plays a dominant role in communication. Both acknowledged that the interpretation of information constitutes that of technology. However, Hall and Ong differed from each other, for the former was aware of the power that governs the interpretation of information and technology.

Ong did not take into account how power shapes the technologies of orality and literacy. He did not ask who can decide for whom how to use certain technologies to communicate with each other. Even though orality may appear to be natural to most humans, the production of speech always takes place in a material form, such as the space where oral exchanges take place. All material forms are shaped by power structure. For example, who are allowed in a space to engage in oral exchanges. Power also shapes writing and printing cultures: not everyone is allowed to own or can afford to own, use, and interpret writing and printing technologies.

The introductory chapter has alluded that in the past, political elites actively prohibited certain populations (such as women, slaves, immigrants) from attaining literacy. Even though some may have functional literacy, the cost of technologies was unaffordable to them, thus denying them opportunities to use and own these technologies. Even though basic literacy has become more widespread and printing technologies have become cheaper, the interpretation of technologies have already been determined by those who have first obtained literacy and owned the means to write and print. For example, newspapers have long been seen as a medium for objective news even though they reflect elite interest (Lewis, 2001). Even though computer software and the Internet enabled those whose voices are left out in mainstream newspapers to publish stories that matter to them, these newspapers are often seen to serve minority interest.

In comparison to Ong's orality/literacy, Hall's encoding/decoding model highlights the power struggle in the production and interpretation of information and technology. In this model, media producers have both the technical competencies and cultural knowledge to choose what news events to cover, package the news events in an appropriate format, and distribute the news packages from television stations to the audience's homes. On the reception side, the audience has fewer choices than the producers: they can choose to watch the news stories or not, and they can use their cultural background to interpret the stories. However, the audiences do not have much power to determine on which technical devices should the news stories be watched. In the old days, it had to be television set. Even in a multi-screen era, the choices are still limited to television, computer and mobile devices. In addition, the audience's understanding of technical devices is shaped by previous experience. For example, news stories on newspapers are expected to be more in-depth than those on television.

After reviewing four influential models of communication, I assert that a communication model that pays attention to power would be more useful to understand information access. In the following, we will ask three questions: How to and who govern information access? How is information access related to public interest? Is the public a racialized concept? As stated in the beginning of the book chapter, if the information access question is simply about whether the public should have access to certain information, then we miss the opportunity to reflect on *who* have the power to decide *for whom* information access. In the next section we move to a more global level to look at how international organizations frame the question of information access.

HOW AND WHO GOVERNS INFORMATION ACCESS?

Governance of information access occurs at many levels: from the local to the global. Some governance is formal, others much less so. At the most local and informal level, parents may restrict Internet access for children because they worry about content or screen time.

Yet, these rules are rarely written down and may not be enforced at all times. At the organizational level, companies may have written rules that govern what information can be shared with whom. Violations of some rules could land employees in troubles or could invite lawsuits. At the global level, international organizations assist national governments, corporations, and non-profit organizations to negotiate information access. Some governance includes hardware provision and infrastructure construction, other relates to training or regulating information ownership.

In this section I focus on the global level and look at how two United Nations agencies—the United Nations Educational, Scientific and Cultural Organization (UNESCO) and the International Telecommunication Union (ITU)—explain why information access is important to the world population, especially citizens in the developing world. These two agencies are chosen because communication is central to their missions. I will first examine their programs about information access, then evaluate whether they see information and technologies as interdependent, and whether they explain information access disparity with power structure.

United Nations Educational Scientific and Cultural Organization (UNESCO)

UNESCO was established after WWII with the belief that world peace could be achieved through international cooperation in education, sciences, and culture. Its expertise in communication and information includes freedom of expression, media development, information access, and building knowledge society. UNESCO stated two reasons why information access is important: first, it counters the negative effect of globalization; second, it builds peaceful and sustainable societies.

UNESCO acknowledges that a side effect of globalization is the marginalization of some communities ("Access to information", n/a). To counter this negative effect, UNESCO advocates national governments and institutions to promote access to information and knowledge, encourage the use of new information and communication technologies, and build multilingual websites. National policies that could increase access are providing Internet access, digital public records, as well as basic computer skills training to citizens. On its "Building knowledge societies" page, UNESCO links information access to world peace, sustainable economic development, and intercultural dialogue. ICTs are essential to achieve these goals because they empower local communities to access, preserve, and share information. In particular, UNESCO highlights that open education materials and open source software would play a role in empowering those who have limited access to information and knowledge ("Building knowledge societies", n/a)

In UNESCO's viewpoint, national governments are the main actors to ensure information access for all citizens, including the disadvantaged ones. It once again advocates member-states to implement national policies to ensure all populations have the computer skills and technological hardware to access online information published in multiple languages.

UNESCO does not seem to pay attention to the interdependent relationship between information and technologies because information is assumed to be "out there" to be accessed. The problem at hand is that citizens do not have the skills and hardware to access it. Its information access programs also assume that digital information, not analogue information, offers a better chance to counter globalization and promote world peace.

International Telecommunication Union (ITU)

The International Telecommunication Union (ITU) was founded in 1865 when radio technology was increasingly used for communication around the world. At the beginning, ITU allocated radio spectrum to users to ensure successful signal transmission. It also standardized Morse code to ensure telegraph communication would use a universal language. At present, ITU continues facilitating international agreements on technologies, services, protocols, and resource allocation such as radio spectrum and satellite orbit positions. ITU also aims to ensure that access to ICTs be affordable, equitable, and universal. Lastly, it believes the world population can be empowered by technological training ("About International Telecommunication Union", n/a).

ITU specifically names three populations that should be better served with new information and communication technologies:

people with disabilities; women and young girls; and youths. For people with disabilities, ITU believes ICTs enable them to access key public services such as healthcare, education and information. Lacking such services will reduce their opportunities in the job market and for independent living (International Telecommunication Union, 2013). It also names a few technological devices that will be the most useful to people with disabilities: web services, mobile devices and services, and television. In comparison, ITU has a different stance towards the use of ICTs among women and young people. It focuses less on information access but more on the job market and the digital economy. It encourages women and young girls to study subjects such as computing science and mathematics so that they would become highly paid professionals. Similarly, it believes that young people's ease with adopting technologies would bring innovation and growth in the ICT sector.

In contrast to UNESCO, ITU focuses on information access for the end goals of employment and economic development. It believes that those who possess ICT skills will secure better jobs. In addition, ICTs will add value to women and youths: women with highly paid jobs and youths with gainful employments would improve the national economy (Sterne & Stabile, 2003). Based on its belief, ITU is not overtly concerned with the interdependent relationship between information and technologies, both are seen as resources for economic advancement.

Do UNESCO and ITU Pay Attention to the Interdependent Relationship Between Technologies and Information? Do They Pay Attention to Power Relations?

In the first section of the book chapter, I examined four models that conceptualize the relationship between information and technologies. I asserted that Shannon and Weaver's transmission model of communication and McLuhan's hot media/cold media model do not pay attention to the interdependent relationship between information and technologies. In addition, these two models, along with Ong's orality/literacy theory, do not take into account how power relations structure who have access to information and technologies. After reviewing how UNESCO and ITU view information access, I argue that neither international organization pays attention to the interdependent relationship between information and technologies. UNESCO believes that the disadvantaged populations can gain knowledge to achieve world peace and a sustainable society as long as they have the skills and technologies to access public information. ITU believes that people with disabilities, women and young girls, as well as young people should exploit information and technologies as potential economic tools to improve their livelihoods. In both cases, information is seen as a resource to be utilized.

In addition, neither UNESCO nor ITU pays attention to how power structure at the local and global levels determines information access. Even though UNESCO has pointed out how globalization marginalizes certain populations, it has not pointed out who facilitates and benefits from globalization. For example, how other international organizations such as the World Intellectual Property Organization advocate that information be seen as private property. Even though UNESCO is right to recognize that digital information can be cheaply reproduced and duplicated for mass distribution, it has not addressed how intellectual property laws have prohibited a lot of materials from being freely distributed. In this sense, the availability of ICTs will not eliminate marginalization. In fact, the blind belief that ICTs would bring information access to all further marginalizes the disadvantaged populations because instead of seeing them as public members, these populations are seen as consumers who need to engage in the digital economy in order to have full information access.

In contrast to UNESCO, ITU is more blatant at stating the market value of ICT skills. It believes that if women and young people are willing to acquire these skills, they will increase their marketability in the job market. In other words, women and young people are like raw, undeveloped materials that need to be worked on so that value can be extracted from them (Lee, 2004). More problematically, ITU did not ask broader questions such as why the unemployment rate of young people is high, who should train young people, and who should benefit from skilled young people. Asking these questions would illuminate the unequal power relations between national governments and transnational corporations. Foreign investors would expect national governments train young people so that they do not have to bear the cost. In addition to foregoing training cost, foreign investors may also demand tax breaks from national governments. All these arrangements mean that national governments need to pay upfront to attract foreign investment because it is seen as a solution to solve youth unemployment problems. These arrangements show the view of ITU is too simplistic: even though skilled young people may improve their economic conditions, transnational corporations exploit both governments and the labor of young people by profiting from them with little investment.

HOW IS PUBLIC INTEREST RELATED TO INFORMATION ACCESS?

In the previous section, I argued that information access will not change the unequal power relationship between disadvantaged populations and transnational corporations if these populations are only seen as workers who produce value for transnational companies. Drastic changes to this power relationship require these populations to see themselves as members of the public, not workers for private entities.

Members of the public enact digital citizenry when they are online. When one exercises digital citizenry, information access would mean effecting social, political, and cultural changes. These changes are essential to foster democracy and to promote justice. Because the concept of digital citizenry has such an importance, I will explore in this section how it relates to that of the public: what is the public? Who belongs to the public? If some members are excluded, is the public a racialized concept? Then I will examine how the public relates to digital citizenry in education and public services contexts. Afterwards I will turn to the U.S. as an example to show even though information regulation has been said to safeguard public interest, regulation often inhibits the public from engaging in a democracy.

What Is the Public? Who Belongs to It?

The questions of what a public is and who belong to it were pondered by American intellectuals. Changes in the American demographics and the rise of the mass media at the turn of the 20th century probed two scholars—Walter Lippmann and John Dewey—to examine what the public is and how information can foster a sense of belonging for this public. Between 1880 and 1920, America's industrial might and economic prosperity attracted immigrants from Central, Eastern, and Southern Europe. These immigrants congregated in cities, very often living in ethnic enclaves. In addition, they were attracted to mass entertainment such as movies and tabloid journalism. Both the influx of immigrants and the rise of mass media created anxieties among intellectuals who tried to grapple how these low-skilled immigrants who speak little English would change democracy in the republic.

Walter Lippmann, a journalist, wrote in a 1922 book *Public opinion* that members of the non-elite class would only receive partial information partly because the mass media had no intention to present accurate information, partly because the readers already brought along their skewed worldview to understand news. Their uncritical interpretation of news reinforced an already biased understanding of news events. Another troubling trend was that Lippmann believed the mass media is successful at presenting a unified worldview, informing the readers that there is a public who shares the same opinion. Therefore, the mass media could be manipulated as a propaganda tool, feeding into readers' prejudiced worldview by providing the opinion of an imagined public.

Lippmann's contemporary, John Dewey, was more optimistic about how information can form a public. In *The public and its problems* (2012), Dewey focused on the relationship between the state—constituted by politicians—and the public. Members of the public are not aware of the membership to the public until the politicians whom they elected fail to fulfill promises. When politicians disappoint their constituencies, members of the public would find a solution, such as finding a common interest among themselves. Information is then essential for the public to find out a common cause and a sound solution.

Even though Lippmann and Dewey conceived their ideas of the public in early 1900s, they are surprisingly applicable to an information-saturated society. For example, Lippmann was correct that the availability of diverse information has not made the public more willing to engage with viewpoints with which they disagree. Instead, they tend to gravitate towards information that reinforces their beliefs (Mothes & Ohme, 2019). Highly tailored news can then feed selective news stories to an already biased reader. Because all these news stories build a cohesive worldview, this biased reader is convinced that the majority of the populations "out there" share the same worldview. Therefore, the availability of information does not necessarily lead to a more informed public.

On the other hand, Dewey was also right about the public seeking common interests. Digital media allow members of the public to form cross-sectional coalitions to influence the political process. Those who do not cross paths in real life can interact with each other online. For example, when President Trump was elected, women of different races, ethnicities, and social classes from all walks of life in different cities quickly organized themselves to stage large-scale protests against the newly elected President's sexist, racist, and homophobic attitudes. They relied on social media to update each other where to meet for marches.

While both Lippmann and Dewey's ideas of a public are still applicable today, it may be worthwhile to compare who formed the public in 1920s and who the online public is today. Dewey believed the public was the voters. In the 1920s, only white men who belonged to certain classes were entitled to vote for their representatives. Even though the Fifteenth Amendment prohibited states from denying black males and poor white males to vote, Jim Crow laws had barred them from voting. Women were only granted the right to vote two years before Lippmann's book was published. Moreover, Native Americans, Chinese immigrants, black men from southern states, and adults under the age of 21 were not given the rights to vote when Lippmann and Dewey wrote about the public. Therefore, the public was a gendered and racialized concept in the 1920s.

However, changes in laws have changed the component of a voting public. Since the 1980s, women voters have been more active than men voters in every presidential election (Center for American Women and Politics, 2019). However, white voters are still more active than non-white voters (McDonald, n/a). While some may suggest that non-white voters, even when given the opportunity, had not exercised their citizens' rights and opt out of the public, data show that non-white Americans tend to have less access to online information. What it means is that if Lippmann and Dewey were right about information access being one condition of participating in the public, then the fact that some populations have more barriers to access online information is *not* because of lacking will and motivation, but lacking economic means to acquire the technologies to access information. For example, in California, African Americans and Latinx who are low-income, less educated, or live in rural areas tend not to have broadband subscriptions at home (Goss, Lee, & Gao, 2019). To these populations, they either rely on handheld devices to access online information or resolve to "traditional" mass media such as television or the radio to receive information. Mass media, according to Lippmann, are not interested in providing diverse viewpoints or a wide spectrum of topics and are therefore not helpful with facilitating a democratic debate. Therefore, lacking technological means to access online information may explain why certain populations cannot fully participate in public life even if they are entitled to a vote.

Digital Citizenry and the Public

In this section I continue the discussion of "digital citizenry" and "public" in two kinds of discourses about information access. The first kind of discourse is the "digital citizenship" movement in school curriculum; the second one is about the homeless population in public libraries. Although these two discourses may appear to be very different, they both reinforce an aforementioned point that the concepts "digital citizenry" and "public" either ignore or exclude populations that do not have reliable means for online access. These discourses effectively see good online citizens as those who have the economic means to acquire technologies. In addition, these technologies are best seen to be consumed in a private home.

The first type of discourse is about an education initiative to promote digital citizenship in schools. Non-profit organizations lobby state governments to ensure that school students use classroom technology safely, become savvy consumers, and develop into proficient content creators (Herold, 2016). A digital citizenship curriculum has a dual focus of preventing negative online experience and promoting positive one. Some common topics that the curriculum touches upon are: internet safety and security; students' digital identities and reputations; appropriate and ethical digital conduct; healthy relationships with technology; cyberbullying; online information sources evaluation; and the ability to access, analyze, produce, evaluate, and interpret a wide range of media. Even though information access through technologies is very often the first and necessary step to enact online citizenship, this step is often neglected in this discourse.

Non-profit organizations that advocate digital citizenship assume school children already have the technologies to access online information so their goal is to guide them through safe use. These organizations conveniently ignored that more than half of the U.S. public school students come from low-income families (Layton, 2015); there are more homeless students in those schools (Camera, 2019); and schools attended by low-income or homeless students are more likely to be poorly funded; lastly, information technologies in these schools tend to be outdated and scarce. To students who experience food and housing insecurities, online access may be a luxury more than a given. The COVID-19 pandemic has illustrated that a large number of school children have no reliable online access and appropriate technology to learn when school buildings are closed.

To illustrate how non-profit organizations take for granted universal information access among school students, I show how Common Sense Media and the International Society for Technology in Education market teaching materials with the concepts "digital citizenship" and "public". Common Sense Media launched a "digital citizenship movement" campaign which promises to make children the top priority of the nation. This campaign stated that school students "have never had as much access to the internet and mobile technologies at home and school as they do today" (Starrett, 2016, para. 2). Therefore, teachers and parents should help them navigate how to use this information. The International Society for Technology in Education believes that digital citizens need to wrestle ethical questions at the intersection of technology and humanity, such as how they can "[use] technology to make your community better; [engage] respectfully online with people who have different beliefs than you; and [use] technology to make your voice heard by public leaders and to shape public policy" ("Digital citizenship in education", n/a). There is little discussion about whether having equitable online access is an ethical question or not.

Further investigation of the funding of Common Sense Media reveals that this non-profit organization receives money from a number of hi-tech, telecommunications, and media corporations such as Apple, ComcastNBCUniversal, AT&T, and DirectTV. It is unknown why these corporations give money to Common Sense Media. One possible reason is that their website recommends to parents movies, television shows, books, apps and games that are safe for their children and these corporations provide the content for review. The review site of Common Sense Media seems to suggest that being an online citizen is being a wise consumer. In an online space, it is the parents' jobs to ensure children are shielded from "bad" content lurking online. This review site has little to do with public life. Instead, it promotes information as a private goods.

The second discourse that shows "online citizenry" and "public" excludes some populations is that of the homeless population in public libraries. Public libraries, by mandate, provide equal information access for all patrons regardless of gender, race, ethnicity, or economic status. However, the discourse about homelessness implies that library patrons who are economically productive are entitled to more freedom to use the library. The homeless are only welcome in public libraries when they use it for information access. This discourse illustrates Foucault's idea of "governmentality" because library policies, news reports, and everyday discourse govern how library patrons should monitor behaviors and appearance of themselves and others.

Public libraries play a wider range of roles when funding to public services is cut. They now offer English classes to immigrants and provide job search services. They are also seen as children's playpens and teenagers' hangouts. In addition, the downtown locations of central branches also provide patrons with facilities such as heating, bathrooms, and indoor seating. As a result, the building provides a comfortable space to homeless populations when shelters are closed during the day. The visibility of homeless populations in public libraries calls into question who has the right to a public space and whether this right conflicts with that of information access. The conflict shows that the acts of accessing information are still done in a physical space even though the immaterial nature of digital information often leads to a misconception that physical space does not matter. Even when a space for information access is acknowledged, this space is assumed to be a private one, such as one's home, dorm room, or office. This space is often not assumed to be in a public space, such as community centers or public libraries.

The conflicts with the right to a public space and with information access are illustrated in the discourse about homeless population in public libraries. While this discourse does not bar the homeless population from gaining access to the building, it also assumes this population is not interested in information access. Therefore, the mere presence of the homeless threatens others' rights to access information. For instance, *The Boston Herald*, a politically conservative newspaper, reported that drug use and fights among homeless people inside the Boston Public Library exert a bad influence on school children (Atkinson, 2017). In a television news report, the newscaster suggested that the homeless do their laundry and sleep in the libraries, implying that they use it improperly (Moroney, 2017). These reports monitoring the behaviors of the homeless by citing their improper use may diminish the rights of the non-homeless.

The discourse of the homeless is so powerful that even the homeless themselves subscribe to the same discourse. For example, *Spare Change News,* a local newspaper that reports about homelessness, wrote that the homeless beat the cold by sinking themselves in "soft reading chairs, warm toilet seats, and in front of computer screens where they watch YouTube, connect to services, and engage in social media" (Alvarez, 2018). Even though the description tries to normalize behaviors by suggesting that what the homeless desire is the same as most populations, this reinforces that the homeless are more likely to *lounge* rather than to actively engage in information-seeking.

The only way to make the homeless more welcome, according to this discourse, is for them to *read a book*: the primary activity associated with the library. For example, a library director was reported to say: "But if someone homeless quietly sits and reads, they won't be bothered" ("Library serves as alternative shelter for homeless", 2019, para. 15). In another instance, one angry patron complained that the homeless waste public money by not taking advantage of reading a book for self-improvement:

> What bothers me the most was not the smell, nor was it the fact that homeless people are in the library. It's the fact that they are sleeping!?!? If you're homeless and in a library . . . READ A BOOK! You've obviously

got nothing better to do with your time, so why not get a little education? . . . Instead, they are busy wasting taxpayer dollars sleeping.
(quoted in Kahn, 2008, para. 18)

The above quote illustrates the view that because the homeless do not economically produce for society, their time is idle. To make themselves more worthy for society, they should better use their time for self-improvement so that they may be able to find a job and lift themselves up.

When the homeless population is visible in a public space, news discourse regulates their behaviors and appearances, exercising what Foucault (see Carroll, 2010) called governmentality: that good citizens should not only follow certain behaviors and appear in certain ways but should also constantly self-monitor themselves. In this discourse, the homeless should make themselves invisible, blend themselves with the non-homeless in by reading a book quietly. If they fail to do so, then they deny others' rights to access information or worse still, endanger public safety.

This discourse, however, does not point out how the non-homeless patrons use the library. For example, in a recent trip to the Boston Public library on a weekday, I saw homeless people watching television shows on their smartphones, but there were also office workers eating lunch in the foyer, nannies feeding babies, and teenagers playing video games on the computers. Despite few actually read a book, the news discourse does not question why the non-homeless populations do not seek self-improvement by absorbing knowledge. As I argued, online citizenry is only reserved for those who can afford technologies, therefore patrons who can buy lunch, parents who can afford a nanny, and teenagers who own a smartphone are those who exhibit good citizenship because they are economically productive members of the society. Therefore, despite the fact that their library use may also be "improper", they are not scrutinized.

The discourses about digital citizenship curriculum and the homeless population in public libraries are strikingly similar. On the surface, both discourses are about information access. But both discourses have an underlying core argument that digital citizenship is only reserved for those who can afford technologies. In addition, both discourses believe public policies should be in place to safeguard digital citizens because of lurking threats to public safety. In the case of digital citizenship, the threat is online content that is not suitable for children; in the case of homelessness and public libraries, the threat to information access is the homeless population. In both discourses, the concepts of online citizenship and the public have been appropriated to mean access to privatized information in a privatized space. In fact, both discourses severely threaten the health of the public and online citizenry.

Relating what Lippmann and Dewey have written about information and the public to a digital age, it seems that the threat to public formation is an unspoken assumption of who can claim online citizenry. Lippmann believed the barriers to this formation are partial information and human psychology; Dewey believed the barrier is the absence of a common cause. In the digital age, it seems that the first barrier is whether one owns the technologies to access information in a private space. If someone does not own the technologies, then they do not have access to information and the ability to connect with others. If this is indeed how online citizenry and the public are understood, then both concepts citizenship and the public are in threat. In the following, I will further show that government regulators also have a narrow view of who constitutes the public.

PUBLIC INTEREST: WHOSE INTEREST DOES IT PROTECT?

In this section, I examine how the U.S. government regulates information access in the name of public interest. At the beginning of the chapter, I used the example of Barack Obama's birth certificate to illustrate that while some believed proof of Obama's birth right is essential to public interest, Obama himself believed it distracts the public from important issues faced by the nation. When both sides claimed their decision is for public interest, who is correct about how information access benefits public interest?

Government agencies regularly use the concept "public interest" to justify why certain policies about information access are made, yet they tend not to define what it is. Adding to the confusion is the lack of uniform policies about information access across media. This lack of uniformity means that while the public is able to access some information from some media, they cannot access the same information from others. This lack of uniformity can be understood by referring to the two arguments that I made at the beginning of the chapter: first, the relationship between information and technology is interdependent; second, those who control the technologies also have a better chance to control information. In the following, I will first examine how three bodies define public interest, then I will suggest how "public interest" relates to the interdependence between technologies and information, lastly I will explain why "public interest" reinforces unequal power relations. The three bodies are a government agency (the U.S. Federal Communications Commission), private entities (Internet service providers), and public libraries.

The Federal Communications Commission (FCC) is an independent government agency that oversees domestic and international telecommunications in all the U.S. states and territories. The domains that FCC regulates are radio, television, wire, satellite, and cable. The FCC does not regulate information access in printed media (such as newspapers, magazines, and books), the Internet, the theater, or DVD releases. The FCC deals with audiences' complaints of obscene, indecent, and profane content. Even though there are distinct definitions of these three types of materials, the FCC admits that the jurisdiction depends on who complain, what the content and context are, as well as when the content is broadcast. For example, indecent and profane content must not be broadcast in the U.S. between 6:00 a.m. and 10:00 p.m., when children may be among the audience. However, this rule only applies to broadcast television and radio, not cable television, satellite television, and satellite radio. What it means is if some grossly offensive comments are made on network television during daytime, parents of young children could file a complaint with the FCC. However, if the same comments are made on cable or satellite television, the FCC will not accept the filing.

This lack of uniformity may not make sense from an audience's perspective because the impact of the content on the audience, regardless of whether it was broadcast on network or cable television, is the same. However, from a regulator's perspective, the regulations to which content is subject should be different because of the technologies through which the content is delivered. Broadcast media—network television, radio—rely on the airwaves. The airwaves are owned by the American public. Because the public owns the airwaves, so the content transmitted through broadcast must take public interest into consideration. In contrast, cable and satellite technologies are privately owned, so public interest is less a consideration.

This case clearly shows the interdependent relationship between information and technologies: information access depends on the technologies through which the information transmits. This case also shows when the technologies are privately owned, the information that passes through them will be less regulated. In other words, public interest is less a concern when the technologies are privately owned.

A similar argument applies to the regulation of information access on the Internet. Because the transmission of Internet data does not rely on public resources, therefore the government is not supposed to interfere with indecent or profane materials online. The audience who are offended by the content instead file their complaints with the content providers. However, content providers have vastly different standards of what kind of information can be shared online. For example, the guidelines of Wikipedia do not mention community standards for obscene, indecent, or profane contents. It only has a section about "child protection" that discourages inappropriate adult–child relationships. On the other hand, YouTube has policies about sexual and violent content, which mirror those of the FCC. For example, YouTube allows nudity *only* if it is for educational, documentary, scientific, or artistic purposes. However, nudity cannot be shown for sexually gratifying purposes. Also similar to FCC policies, YouTube outlaws obscene materials (such as child pornography) and will report content that contains child sexual abuse imagery to law enforcement.

The confusing regulations of media and online content may lead some to advocate for uniform policies. Because the U.S. only regulates content when it is transmitted through public resources, so uniform policies necessitates seeing technologies as public goods. In 2015, President Obama announced that Internet Service Providers (ISPs) should be seen as quasi-governmental public utilities that will be subject to more government regulations (Downes, 2015). In other words, broadband Internet should be seen as more like water and electricity, they are necessities for modern living. If ISPs are regulated like other public utilities, then the government will oversight operations, investment in facilities and services, pricing as well as customer interaction.

However, corporations and business-friendly politicians have been strongly opposed to policies that count broadband technologies as public utilities. They believe that government regulations will hurt competition. They also believe that unfettered competition between companies will achieve the best services and prices for customers. The counter-argument does not take into consideration the interdependent relationship between ownership of technologies and content regulation. It mainly sees technologies as conduits to transmit content.

Another complication about public interest and information access is that the setting of information access matters. In principle, Internet users can access any online information (including the indecent or profane one) as long as the content does not offend anyone who may accidentally see it. Few settings afford such absolute freedom. Except for a private home, public settings (such as school, public libraries, community centers, public transportation) and some private settings (such as the workplace, private clubs) have explicit policies about what kind of information access is restricted. For example, the Internet Policy of the Boston Public Library stated that patrons may not "receive or display graphics which may reasonably be construed as obscene as defined by law" ("Internet policy", n/a). As I have demonstrated in an earlier section, the public in the context of public libraries excludes patrons that have little economic power. If a male homeless person is found watching an educational video with nudity (such as childbirth) in a public library, the chance of other patrons being offended is probably higher than a well-dressed pregnant woman watching the same video in the same setting. This example shows that not only are technologies and information interdependent, but the setting in which these technologies are available also matters to information access. Even if a setting is deemed public, those who are deemed members of the public also matters to information access.

CONCLUSION

At the beginning of this chapter, I used Barack Obama's birth certificate controversy to illustrate that if the question concerning information access is only about public interest, then we will miss opportunities to examine how unequal power relations shape the discourse of information access. Many examples illustrate the following four questions:

first, whether technologies and information are interdependent; second, how to and who govern information access; third, how information access is related to public interest; and fourth, whether the public is a racialized and class-based concept.

First, I examined four influential communication models and asked if they have taken into account the interdependent relationship between technologies and information. Shannon and Weaver's transmission model of communication and McLuhan's "hot/cold media" did not acknowledge this interdependent relationship: while the former privileges information, the latter technologies. The transmission model of communication is more interested in understanding how information can effectively transmit from the sender to the receiver. On the other hand, the "hot/cold" media model suggests that the technologies determine how the audience understand information. In comparison, Walter Ong's orality/literacy and Stuart Hall's encoding/decoding models take into account the interdependent relationship between technologies and information, that there is a mutually constitutive relationship between interpretation of information and technologies. Between the two, only Hall's encoding/decoding model asks how those control technologies also control the interpretation of information.

Next, I examined how three international organizations (UNESCO, ITU, and the World Bank) explained the importance of information access for the disadvantaged populations in developing countries. These three organizations assume that information is independent of technologies: as long as the disadvantaged population has access to technologies, they can make good use of it. Among the three organizations, ITU and the World Bank approach information access with a neoliberal agenda; they believe young women and unemployed youths should be trained to produce information so that they contribute to the economies of their families and countries. Under this neoliberal agenda, disadvantaged populations have little value to transnational companies. Knowledge about digital technologies, however, will transform them into valuable resources for foreign investors and transnational corporations. This neoliberal agenda thus reinforces the unequal relations between transnational companies and countries, between populations that own technologies and those that don't.

Next I argue that the concept of "public" does not include all members of the public. The discussion about information access and public formation in the 1920s still applies to that about online citizenry a century later. I examined how two intellectuals—Walter Lippmann and John Dewey—explained the formation of public as a result of information in the early 20th century. Lippmann believed that the mass media inclined to give partial information to a mass audience that had no desire to learn diverse viewpoints. Dewey believed that diverse information helps different groups to find common interests at times of political discontent. To both, the concept of the public closely tied to the electorate, which, at that time, excluded women, people of color, and recent immigrants.

A century after Lippmann and Dewey wrote about the American public, the online citizenry discourse continues to exclude some members of the public, specifically the populations that do not have the economic means to own technological devices. The discourse about online citizenry curriculum has conveniently ignored the large number of low-income and homeless students who do not have access to digital technologies at home. The discourse is more about protecting children from harmful online materials. In addition, the discourse about the homeless population in public libraries implies that the presence of the homeless in a public space diminishes others' opportunities to access information. Once again, children's safety is used as a reason to explain why the homeless are not welcome in public libraries. Both discourses legitimize the unequal relations in a digital society: this society is not open to all, only those who already have the economic means to purchase technologies and use them in a private space.

Lastly, I argue that information access policies in the U.S. well illustrate the interdependent relationship between information and technologies. Even though public interest has been used as a reason to justify why indecent and profane materials should be inaccessible to all members of the public, some media have more freedom to distribute these materials. For example, broadcast media are the strictest, followed by cable and satellite television, and the Internet. The reason why there lacks a uniform policy is because of the technologies through which information is transmitted. Broadcast media rely on a public resource—the airwaves—for signal transmission, therefore broadcasters are subject to government oversight. On the other hand, the Internet is a self-regulated medium, different content providers have different guidelines of what can or cannot be shown. An obvious solution to standardize guidelines of indecent and profane content is to see broadband services as public services. However, a proposal of making it a public resource has been strongly opposed by large corporations and conservative politicians. They believe that public broadband services reduce the competitiveness of the market, thus leading to poor services for consumers. This argument sees public interest as that of consumers and the market is seen as the best place to serve this public. Similar to the discourses about online citizenry and the homeless populations, this argument appropriated the concept "public" and limited it to consumers who could afford technologies.

BIBLIOGRAPHY

About FCC. (n/a). Federal Communications Commission. Retrieved from: https://www.fcc.gov/about/overview

About International Telecommunication Union (ITU). (n/a). ITU. Retrieved from: https://www.itu.int/en/about/Pages/default.aspx

Access to information. (n/a). UNESCO. Retrieved from: https://en.unesco.org/themes/access-information

Alvarez, N. (2018, January 23). Bitter sleep: An incident at the Boston Public Library. *Spare Change News*. Retrieved from: http://sparechangenews.net/2018/01/bitter-sleep-incident-boston-public-library/

Atkinson, D. (2017, September 29). Libraries beset by violence, addicts in restrooms. *Boston Herald*. Retrieved from: https://www.bostonherald.com/2017/09/29/libraries-beset-by-violence-addicts-in-restrooms/

Building knowledge societies. (n/a). UNESCO. Retrieved from: https://en.unesco.org/themes/building-knowledge-societies

Camera, L. (2019, February 21). Number of homeless. *U.S. News*. Retrieved from: https://www.usnews.com/news/education-news/articles/2019-02-21/number-of-homeless-students-soars

Carroll, A. P. (2010). Come as you are: Negotiating neoliberal governmentality at a homeless shelter for women and children (master's thesis). University of British Columbia, Vancouver, Canada.

Center for American Women and Politics. (2019). *Gender differences in voter turnout*. New Brunswick, NJ: Rutgers University. Retrieved from: https://www.cawp.rutgers.edu/sites/default/files/resources/genderdiff.pdf

Daniels, J. (2009). *Cyber racism: White supremacy online and the new attack on civil rights*. Lanham, MD: Rowman and Littlefield.

Dewey, J. (2012). *The public and its problems: An essay in political inquiry*. University Park, PA: Pennsylvania State University Press.

Digital citizenship in education. (n/a). International Society for Technology in Education. Retrieved from: https://www.iste.org/learn/digital-citizenship

Downes, L. (2015, September 9). Judgment Day for the FCC's latest net neutrality folly. *Forbes*. Retrieved from: https://www.forbes.com/sites/larrydownes/2015/09/09/judgment-day-for-the-fccs-latest-net-neutrality-folly/#600fa839ab38

Evans, M. (2016). Information dissemination in new media: YouTube and the Israeli–Palestinian conflict. *Media, War and Conflict, 9*(3), 325–343.

Fiske, J. (1982). *Introduction to communication studies*. London: Routledge

Fuddy, L. J. (2011, April 25). State of Hawaii Department of Health. Correspondence with the White House. Retrieved from: https://obamawhitehouse.archives.gov/sites/default/files/rss_viewer/birth-certificate-correspondence.pdf

Goss, J., Lee, C., & Gao, N. (2019, March). California's digital divide. *Public Policy Institute of California*. Retrieved from: https://www.ppic.org/publication/californias-digital-divide/

Hall, S. (1992). Encoding, decoding. In S. During (Ed.), *The cultural studies reader* (pp. 90–103). London: Routledge.

Herold, B. (2016, October 28). K-12 digital citizenship initiative targets states. *Education Week*. Retrieved from: https://www.edweek.org/ew/articles/2016/10/28/k-12-digital-citizenship-initiative-targets-states.html

International Telecommunication Union. (2013). *The ICT opportunity for a disability-inclusive development framework*. Geneva, Switzerland: ITU.

Internet policy. (n/a). Boston Public Library. Retrieved from: https://www.bpl.org/about-us/official-policies/internet-policy/

Kahn, R. (2008, June 15). Free to all. *Boston Globe*. Retrieved from: http://archive.boston.com/news/local/massachusetts/articles/2008/06/15/free_to_all/?page=full

Layton, L. (2015, January 16). Majority of U.S. public school students are in poverty. *Washington Post*. Retrieved from: https://www.washingtonpost.com/local/education/majority-of-us-public-school-students-are-in-poverty/2015/01/15/df7171d0-9ce9-11e4-a7ee-526210d665b4_story.html

Lee, M. (2004). UNESCO's conceptualization of women and telecommunications 1970–2000. *Gazette: The International Journal for Communication Studies, 66*(6), 533–552.

Lewis, J. (2001). *Constructing public opinion: How political elites do what they like and why we seem to go along with it*. New York: Columbia University Press.

Library serves as alternative shelter for homeless. (2019, March 11). *WHDH.com*. Retrieved from: https://whdh.com/news/library-serves-as-alternative-shelter-for-homeless/

McDonald, M. P. (n/a). Voter turnout demographics. *United States election projects*. Retrieved from: http://www.electproject.org/home/voter-turnout/demographics

McLuhan, M. (1994). *Understanding media: The extensions of man*. Cambridge, MA: MIT Press.

Moroney, J. (2017, September 19). Number of homeless and people doing drugs prompts concerns at Boston Public Library. *NBC Boston*. Retrieved from:

https://www.nbcboston.com/news/local/number-of-homeless-and-people-doing-drugs-prompts-concerns-at-boston-public-library/29135/

Mothes, C., & Ohme, J. (2019). Partisan selective exposure in times of political and technological upheaval: A social media field experiment. *Media and Communication*, 7(3), 42–53.

Ong, W. (2002). *Orality and literacy: The technologizing of the word*. New York: Routledge.

Pfeiffer, D. (2011, April 27). President Obama's long form birth certificate. The White House blog. Retrieved from https://obamawhitehouse.archives.gov/blog/2011/04/27/president-obamas-long-form-birth-certificate

Robertson, J. W. (2007). TV news: Do they mean us? Television news is the most widely accessed and the most trusted source of current affairs information. But is our trust in it misplaced? *Sociology Reviews*, 17(1), 6–10.

Smith, B., & Tau, B. (2011, April 22). Birtherism: Where it all began. *Politico*. Retrieved from: https://www.politico.com/story/2011/04/birtherism-where-it-all-began-053563

Starrett, JR. (2016, July 15). The digital citizenship movement: The next big legislative trend? Common Sense Kids action. Retrieved from: https://www.commonsensemedia.org/kids-action/blog/the-digital-citizenship-movement-the-next-big-legislative-trend

Sterne, J., & Stabile, C. (2003). Using women as middle men: The promise of ICTs. *Feminist Media Studies*, 3(3), 364–368.

von Baeyer, H. C. (2004). *Information: The new language of science*. Cambridge, MA: Harvard University Press.

5
USING

INTRODUCTION

In Chapter 3, "Searching", we looked at how higher education institutions and libraries define "information literacy". In this chapter we look at how organizations use information to advance their missions, such as advancing benefits for the public and consumers. In Chapter 3, one definition of "information literacy" is an *individual*'s ability to realize a need for, access, evaluate, and use information in a context-appropriate and socially responsible manner. This definition of information literacy, however, does not concern how organizations, such as governments and corporations, use information. This definition also does not consider the social and political consequences of information use in institutions. In this chapter, I suggest that understanding how and why organizations use information is important because organizations have more power than most individuals.

Most organizations have more power than individuals because they have more resources to collect information and to decide how it is used. For example, governments use information to understand citizens' needs so that they can provide adequate public resources; corporations use information to understand consumers' behaviors so that they can provide better goods and services. However, organizations' power over information also means they can decide how to spend money and resources to collect, analyze, and apply information. For example, governments carry out census to gather residents' information, corporations hire data scientists to analyze data. Because of their power, organizations can use information to achieve political and economic goals, such as determining funding allocation for infrastructure and education or what products to manufacture.

Despite the good intentions, ultimately governments and corporations use information to control different populations which may result in unequal and inequitable resource distribution. For example, allocation of education funding determines school quality, but some districts get more money than others; decisions to make certain goods may exclude some consumers or change their consumption habits. More dangerously, when political and economic power intertwines, governments and corporations can control citizens and consumers more effectively. For example, districts with better schools attract higher-income residents who drive up housing prices. Higher housing prices push out low-income residents who have fewer choices with schools. Higher housing prices mean that there will be grocery stores with a wider range of food; low-income areas may become food deserts where residents have little access to perishable food. In addition, high living costs also mean poorly paid service workers spend a long time to commute to work in wealthier area, resulting in poor life quality.

Despite the tremendous control that governments and corporations have over information, the public tends to pay more attention to policies that deal with data privacy and cybersecurity than those about political, social, and economic equality and equity. For example, the U.S. census ensures that individual identity is protected, but the information collected does not ensure equitable resource allocation. To this date, the U.S. census does not have racial categories of Middle Eastern or North Africa. Populations who self-identity as Middle Eastern or North African are forced to choose between white or Other. Not having such racial categories means these populations are less likely to complete the census (Gupta, 2020). Consequently they are undercounted and do not receive funding allocated to them. Likewise, companies ensure that customers' information will not be shared, but it does not guarantee that they will not use information to discriminate against low-income populations (Waddell, 2016).

Because of the tremendous power that organizations have over information and because resource allocation may not be equitable, a critical perspective is needed to examine how the use and control of information creates gender and race bias. A critical perspective will show how power influences public and social lives. As lenses of analysis, race and gender are more than an examination of whether information use is the same across races and genders, but how the working of power produces differentiated experiences of information for people with different backgrounds and life experiences. The race and gender lenses aim to unmask how the exercise of power—either intentionally or unintentionally—systematically excludes certain populations from fully participating in social and civic lives and from benefiting from social goods. Based on the above discussion, this book chapter asks four key questions.

How Is the Use of Information Gender-, Race-, and Class-Biased?

The above discussion has shown that information gathered from census enables policy-makers to decide funding allocations of public goods. These decisions are often race- and gender-biased. To use the example of school quality and housing price, low-income families—that are more likely headed by a single female parent—have fewer opportunities to choose a good school not only because of their limited economic power to choose where they live, but also because they have much less influence on how census information is used to determine funding.

Advanced technologies also enable governments to gather more information from its citizens (Braman, 2006). "Intelligent" national identity cards are said to be technologies that help governments understand citizens' needs better. For example, citizens will have faster and better access to public services. However, some also question whether this surveillance technology acts as control points from the government. For example, a family who fails to pay taxes may be quickly denied access to social services because government agencies have access to information of all citizens. When national identity cards are coupled with facial recognition technologies and camera surveillance, the government has the power to track every citizen's movement.

However, the wealthiest populations have more freedom to escape from state surveillance by spending time in their yachts, private jets, or foreign countries.

How Does the Military Use Information for Intelligence and Combat?

Information is central to warfare. Modern wars are information wars. We will look at how information was used for communication, control, and command (CCC) in the First Gulf War and the War on Terror. The First Gulf War (1990–1991) was called an information war because command was made thousands of miles away through the computer screen. The Second Gulf War (2003–2011) exemplified the importance of information in decision-making. The capture and killing of Osman Bin Laden in Pakistan was monitored in the White House remotely. The War on Terror, in comparison, was a misinformation war. The attack of the Twin Towers had sparked Islamophobia in the U.S. and abroad. Muslims have been scapegoated as dangerous, religious fanatics. Misinformation, however, is not new: propaganda was widely used in the two world wars and the Vietnam War. However, the 2016 U.S. Presidential election popularized the terms misinformation, disinformation, and fake news. The social media have been blamed as a vehicle for foreign governments to influence the opinions of U.S. voters.

What Are Big Data? How Do Corporations Use Big Data to Select "High-Value" Consumers?

Big Data has become a buzzphrase in the business world and some non-profit industries. Advanced information technologies made Big Data possible because powerful machines can process a large amount of data. While Big Data is said to enable corporations to make better decisions, these decisions often benefit certain consumers than others. In addition, Big Data technology and the data are proprietary, they are not available in the public domain. In order to show how proprietary data benefit business goals while limiting consumers' choices and undercutting competitors, we will look at the cases of Amazon and Netflix.

INFORMATION GATHERING BY THE GOVERNMENTS

How can governments collect information about its citizens? It is a much less straightforward process than one would imagine, especially in countries where information collection is decentralized. In contrast, some other countries use a centralized approach by issuing smart identity cards. Such move has created resistance among citizens because of privacy concerns by linking personal identification with sensitive information (Gandy, 1993).

Information collection in the U.S. is relatively decentralized with different agencies collecting different information. The U.S. census is only one but many ways to collect demographic information. Other agencies that collect information are the Internal Revenue Service (IRS) that collects information about personal income and company revenue, the Department of Motor Vehicles (DMV) that collects information about drivers and vehicles, and City Hall that issues and stores birth certificates, marriage licenses, and death certificates. However, a long-term resident may have no record in the U.S. For example, immigrants can leave no record with government authorities if they enter the U.S. without going through border checkpoints, taking up jobs from employers who do not record payment, and not having a driver's licence.

To ensure reliable record-keeping, some governments issue smart identity cards with a unique number to identify every resident. Such number is tied to taxation, healthcare services, and public records. Citizens in some countries, however, resist being issued with a smart identity card due to privacy reasons. For example, the U.K. national identity card was only in place for four years. The scheme was repealed because of civil liberty concerns. The case of mainland China may be the most extreme: together with the Resident Identity Card, facial recognition technologies and closed circuit cameras in public places aid authority to effectively track and identify residents who exhibit improper or illegal behavior in public.

Whether governments choose decentralized or centralized methods of information collection and record-keeping, there are implications on gender and race. In the following, we first review the racial bias of the U.S. Census from the earliest era of the republic to the present days.

How the U.S. Census Classified Race

The U.S. census is racially biased. Yet it enjoys an authoritative status of documenting U.S. demographic change. At the very beginning, race was seen as a biological attribute and the census workers were the ones who decided the race of the household members. Even though race is now self-reported and household members could choose "others" as an option, the "white" race is still seen as the norm because this racial category is rarely questioned.

The first U.S. census took place in 1790. The newly formed U.S. Congress asked the marshals of the U.S. judicial districts to visit every household to collect information which would be shared with the President. The purpose of the census was to determine how much tax was to be collected from states and how many political representatives would represent the states. The first census only had two questions: the name of the head of the family and the number of persons in each household. The residents in each household were classified into five types: free white males over the age of 16; free white males under the age of 16; free white females; all other free peoples; and slaves ("1790 overview", n/a). A quick scan of the names of the heads of the household shows that overwhelmingly the majority were male names. The ordering of the classification from male to female, from free to enslaved also reflected gender and racial hierarchies. Even though the census named the race white, it did not name the race black, they were either "all other free peoples" or "slaves". In addition, not all persons bore the same weight: free persons were counted as one and all other persons (including slaves) were counted as three-fifths (Wright, 1900). The three-fifth of a person was a compromise between the Southern states and the Northern states. While Southern states wanted to count slaves as a whole person because they wanted to increase state representatives, Northern states did not want to count slaves as persons (Philbrick, 2018). The decision was, however, about how white elites wielded more power for themselves, it was not a decision made by slaves. Also, Native Americans (then called Indians) were omitted because they were not to be taxed. Both cases show that the purpose of the census was mainly for political and taxation reasons rather than for statistical ones.

The 1850 U.S. census added a slave questionnaire. The owners were to list the slaves and each of them was assigned a number. If the slaves were sold to new owners, then the number were re-assigned. In addition, owners were to report the number of escaped and freed slaves ("1850", n/a).

The introduction of the 1860 census included an analysis of the African American population because slave trade was abolished. The census also speculated the changes in slave and free colored populations. The motivations behind the analysis and the speculation seemed to be more how changes in African American population would have implications on the white race: "the relative increase of the whites exceeds that of the colored, and that the disparity is gradually [...] more and more favorable to this part of our population" (Kennedy, 1864, p. ix). The analysis struck a triumphant tone about the rising number of whites; the growing number of whites was believed to be essential to maintain the vitality of the human race. This shows that not all humans were considered equal.

Even though the writer of the 1860 census was sympathetic towards freed slaves, the report also exhibited deeply some prejudiced views of blacks. For example, the author believed that freed slaves had made significant progress despite, he claimed, the fact that "[this] race [was] forcibly transported to a state of slavery here, from a country without history, literature or laws, whose people remain in barbarism" (Kennedy, 1864, p. xi). The report also hinted at an increased number of mixed-race children born to black mothers. However, the author failed to mention the circumstances under which black women were impregnated by white males. The writer's attitude was that mixed-race children are inferior so the increased number of them raised some concerns (Brown, 2020). The report further speculated how mixed races may challenge the future of blacks: "the mulattoes have multiplied excessively in the condition of freedom in the northern States; [... but] the mulattoes have had greatly the preference over the pure blooded Africans" (p. x). At that point, who were counted as pure-blooded Africans and who were counted as mixed was a judgment call from census workers who filled in the survey. For the 1920 census, it was reported that when the census worker was a "negro", then there were more counts of "mulattoes" probably due to their care to make the distinction (Bureau of the Census, 1921).

The conclusion of the Civil War also put to an end of "slave questionnaire" that commenced in 1850. The 1870 Census started to count

Native Americans as part of the U.S. population. Their taxation status no longer excluded them from the general population. Instead, they should be reported "just as truly as the vagabond or pauper of the white or the colored race" (Walker, 1872, p. xvi). The census report further suggested that any Native American should be "recognized as a human being" in a census that even counted the number of cattle and horses (ibid.). However, not all Native Americans were seen as "real" Americans, only those who broke tribal relations were believed to enter the U.S. society. The report also had a problem with "half-breeds"—namely, mixed-raced Native Americans. It questioned whether the "superior" or "inferior" blood (p. xiii) should be counted. Even though it did not specify what superior blood means, it likely meant those having white ancestors. In the end, whiteness was defined as how much Native Americans culturally assimilated themselves. Those who adopted whites' manners and trades would be counted as whites.

The classification of race changed from one decade to the next, but the "white" race remained the only constant. In 1860, the California census added Chinese as a race. The 1870 federal census had "Chinese" as a race but this designation also included other Asians immigrants. The race was added because of an increased number of Chinese arriving the U.S. to work on the railroad (Brown, 2020). Similar to how the census surveyed blacks and Native Americans, it also kept an eye on the growth and distribution of Chinese. Census enumerators would go to Chinese households and businesses and ask for registration evidence or else the Chinese would be deported (McGlinn, 1991).

In the 1890 and 1900 censuses, all non-whites were called colored. The largest group of this population was "persons of negro descent" which was further classified into "negros" (100 percent blacks), "mulattoes" (half-blacks), "quadroons" (one-quarter black), and "octoroons" (one-eighth black). Even though "quadroons" and "octoroons" have more white blood than black, they were still classified as colored. Other "colored" populations were Chinese, Japanese (added as a category in 1890), and civilized Indians. The reports did not explain why the races of Chinese and Japanese were added. They were also not too concerned about the implications of Chinese and Japanese populations on whites as much as that of blacks on whites.

One speculation is that there were few mixed-race children between Asians and whites.

The term "colored" was dropped from the 1910 census. The populations were classified into white, negro, Indian, Chinese, Japanese, and all others. Twenty years later, in 1930, these categories were reduced to three: "white", "negro", and "other races". The last category included a wide range of races, such as Mexican, Indian (Native American), Chinese, Japanese, Filipino, Hindu, Korean, Hawaiian, Malay, Siamese (Thai), and Samoan. Mexicans were now included as a race because of an increased number between 1920 and 1930. They arrived the U.S. because of state violence and a weakened economy in Mexico. They were also attracted to mining and agricultural jobs in the American Southwest. In prior censuses, Mexicans were counted as whites. In 1950, races were simplified into "whites" and "nonwhites". As suggested, the only constant in the census was the white race.

The 1960 census had a major breakthrough, it relied on self-reported data rather than observations from the census-takers. It also redefined race as something not biological and not clear cut. In the 1970 census, the classification of Mexican was replaced by persons with Spanish origins; namely, persons who self-identified their origins from Mexico, Puerto Rica, Cuba, Central or South America. The more contemporary terms Latinx or Hispanic were not used until 1980. The 1980 census used ethnic identifications similar to contemporary use. The categories were: persons with Spanish origin; Black persons; American Indians, Eskimos, and Aluet persons; Asian and Pacific Island persons.

In the 2000 census, race was finally recognized as a self-identified sociopolitical construct. Race was rejected as merely scientific or anthological. The term hispanic or Latino replaced "persons with Spanish origin" and was not listed as a race. The five races then became: White; Black or African American; American Indian and Alaska Native; Asian; and Native Hawaiian and other Pacific Islander. Respondents could also choose "some other race" or "two or more races". In addition, instead of having one race per household, the 2010 census also allowed each individual in a household to self-identify his/her race.

Gupta (2020) asserted that up until the 1950s, the question about race was not about racial integration or equality, but more about justifying unjust discrimination against people of color (Gupta, 2020). The census appeared to be an objective instrument that measures changes in populations but its history shows that it was biased towards the non-white populations. The census determined who could be counted as a whole person, how races were named and classified. Lastly, the census was a surveillance technique to speculate how the non-white populations would bring negative consequences to the vitality of the white race which was seen to be essential to the health of the nation. Even though the census has now accepted that race is a social construct, it still does not problematize the white race.

Functions of the U.S. Census

The U.S. Census was launched for taxation and political representations purposes, but they are also important historical documents that show a nation's changing attitudes towards non-dominant races. Even though it is easy to suggest that society has made significant strides towards inclusion by recognizing that race is socially constructed rather than biologically determined, it is difficult to suggest the census promotes racial equality or racial justice. First, many advocates have suggested that rigid racial classification does not reflect populations' racial and ethnic identifications; second, some populations tend not to fill in the census in fear of government action; third, census has been used for decision-making that has implications on racial relations.

Since the 2000 census, race has been seen as a self-identification; some may identify with the nationality of origin, others with ethnicity. The census defines origins as heritage, nationality, lineage, country of birth of the person or the person's parents or ancestors. The 2000 census was also the first one in which an individual can self-identify as mixed race (Brown, 2020). The census continued to not see hispanic as a race; those who self-identify with Hispanic, Latinx, or Spanish may choose any race. The five races remain: White; Black or African American; American Indian or Alaska Native; Asian; Native Hawaiian and Pacific Islander. There is also a write-in box for those who do not identify with any of the five races.

Even though the 2020 US Census has a more fluid view of race, its understanding of race is critiqued to be not relativist enough, in particular for first generation immigrants. For example, historically the

U.S. census sees individuals with any black heritage as black rather than white. However, mixed-race individuals in some other countries (such as Cuba) believe any white heritage will make them white (Gupta, 2020). In addition, even though white has been the constant racial classification since the beginning of the census, modern genome sequencing reveals individuals' biological make up (see also Chapter 2, "Defining"). Some individuals who have long seen themselves as white have found out they may be mixed-race. This new finding allowed them to check the "non-white" box. In addition, people may change their racial identification from one census to another: millions who identified as multiracial in 2000 decided that they are single race a decade later (McGinty, 2020). While genome sequencing and self-identification may appear to show that race has always been a social construct, not every single individual enjoys the same degree of freedom to choose their race. As shown, census-takers had long been the ones who decided the race for others. Even though now individuals can self-identify their race, in daily lives they are still perceived by others to belong to certain races.

The Census suggested that statistics about race help federal agencies monitor compliance with anti-discrimination provisions. However, a large number of individuals fail to return the census for a few reasons. First, some stop responding to the census when there are questions that confuse them. For example, people who believe Hispanic is a race may find it confusing why it is not considered to be one (NALEO Educational Fund, 2019). In addition, people with origins in the Middle East and North Africa may not identify as being "white" (Gupta, 2020). Second, census respondents are assumed to be U.S. residents who have a somewhat stable home address. This assumption excludes the homeless populations, deployed troops, college students, incarcerated people, and displaced people (Wang, 2019). Third, some populations—such as recent residents who have not yet attained citizenship or undocumented immigrants—tend not to respond to the census in fear of government action. In 2020, the Trump administration had attempted to add a question about citizenship in the census but it was blocked by the Supreme Court (Wang, 2019). If this question had been added, the response rate would probably have been much lower because some respondents would have feared being deported. When a large number of residents fail to fill in the census, it will lead to undercounting in some areas, such as urban areas where immigrants tend to settle (Totenberg & Wang, 2019).

Information about race in the census has implications on political decisions, which in turn shape racial relations. On the positive side, data on the census help reveal persistent disparities rooted from historical racial and ethnic discrimination (NALEO Educational Fund, 2019). On the negative side, who gets counted is motivated by white politicians' desire to consolidate more power for themselves. How populations are counted have been manipulated for political cause. At the very beginning, law-makers argued over whether slaves should be counted in the census. The southern states wanted to inflate their number of political representatives so they wanted slaves to be counted; but the northern states did not. In contemporary time, if a race is made visible, then populations that belong to this race are likely to receive federal funding. Therefore, even though Hispanics is not a race but the population is still made visible because there is a hispanic classification (Gupta, 2020). In contrast, populations who identify as Middle Eastern and North African descent are counted as whites so they do not receive specific funding. It has also been found that census tends to undercount black males because of incarceration and premature deaths. Black children were also undercounted (Runes, 2019). On the contrary, there is an overcounting of non-Hispanic white individuals. The discrepancy leads to less funding allocated for black communities and more for white communities.

NATIONAL IDENTITY CARDS

The U.S. census has the dual purpose of designating the number of political representatives in the House of Representatives and allocating funding to different constituents. However, problems such as mismatched racial identifications and underreported minority populations have cast doubts on the reliability of U.S. census data. A more accurate way to track populations and to estimate their needs may be national identity cards and numbers. In some countries, an identity card is required to open bank accounts, apply for jobs, and receive medical care. However, national identity cards and numbers are controversial because they increase the state's surveillance and control of citizens (Roberts & Webster, 1988). The acceptance or rejection of state surveillance also reflects on citizens' trust in the government.

The Japanese government implemented a My Number ID card scheme in 2016 for the purposes of taxation and social security. The government argues that the ID card will increase efficiency of providing social services because different agencies can access the same database ("ID system raises thorny issues", 2013). The number was later connected to citizens' bank account so that the government could detect cases of tax evasion ("Valid concerns over My Number", 2015). Some common objections to such an integrated database are data leaking, identity theft, and cybersecurity. Others deem national identification numbers unconstitutional because such a scheme would increase the government's control over a large amount of personal information, including something as personal as health information and career history (Osaki, 2015). The scheme also has a gender bias: it forces a couple to choose one family name; usually it is the married woman who would use a husband's name rather than her maiden name even though her documents are registered with her maiden name (Aoki, 2016).

The United Kingdom introduced a national identity card in 2005 but the scheme was terminated in 2010. The government proposed to issue a national identity card in the wake of 9/11 terrorist attacks when passengers could board planes without passports ("Timeline: ID cards", 2010). The government also believed that a national identity card would prevent misuse of public resources. The scheme was terminated because the public did not have faith in the government for keeping the data secure, collecting personal and biometric information, and violating civil liberties (McCarthy, 2015). However, the public did not seem to be too concerned when foreign nationals residing in the U.K. are required to have an identity card that contains biometric information (Travis, 2010). However, the identity card was also believed to be proof of someone's legal status, particularly for Caribbean immigrants who moved to the U.K. without being assigned a U.K. passport. Now these immigrants have no national document to prove their legal status to receive public services (Mathieson, 2018). Power once again plays a part in launching and terminating the scheme. While the government wanted such a scheme to better survey potential terrorists who are assumed to be non-U.K. citizens, the worries about civil liberty violation led to the scheme's termination. The termination, however, was at the expense of Caribbean immigrants whose citizenship could have been recognized with such a scheme.

Both Japan and United Kingdom run on a democratic political system so citizens may be more aware of privacy rights and civil liberty. In contrast, citizens in the People's Republic of China are subject to a much higher level of state surveillance. Chinese nationals in mainland China are required to have an identity card when they reach the age of 16. The ID card is required to obtain residence permits and driving licences, open bank accounts, check into hotels, buy high-speed railway tickets, and board domestic flights (Tao, 2018). The ID card can easily track citizens' movements inside the country. In addition, China is building a facial recognition system and surveillance camera network that can track individuals' movements and actions in public places. The government argues that the system was developed to track wanted suspects (Chen, 2017). However, given China's poor track record of human rights, state surveillance technology may be used to identify human rights activists. There were also instances that local authority used surveillance technology to publicly shame residents for behaviors such as wearing pyjamas, lying down, and playing cards in public. Residents who act in an "uncivilized" manner will have their names and identity numbers displayed in public (Van Boom, 2010). While the local residents did express outrage at privacy intrusion at the local governments, few are openly concerned about state surveillance at the national level. However, how citizens feel about such state surveillance may not be known given China's past records of punishing those who criticize the government.

INFORMATION WARFARE: HOME AND ABROAD

In the previous section, I examined how governments collect citizen information for resource allocation and for population control. In this section, I examine how governments use information to control what citizens think about certain issues. In some cases, they also attempt to influence how citizens of other nations think about their own governments.

Schemes to control how citizens think have many labels but most of them are negative, such as propaganda, misinformation, disinformation, and information warfare. A lot has been written about how information has been used in warfare, so this chapter focuses on the First Gulf War—commonly called the first information war—and the War on Terror—legitimized by misinformation about Muslims. I will conclude this section by discussing how social media have become a vehicle through which one government can influence opinions of citizens in other countries.

The First Gulf War (1990–1991) was led by a multi-country coalition to free Kuwait from Iraqi occupation. Iraq conquered its neighbour Kuwait seeking to take over its oil reserves. Western countries worried that Iraq would next attack Saudi Arabia, another major oil exporter. If Iraq had successfully done so, then it would have controlled the majority of oil reserves in the world. Unlike previous wars, the U.S.-led coalition used a wider range of communication technologies to avoid casualties on its side: the coalition was attributed to "the collection, dissemination, and application of information and knowledge" (Mann, 1994, para. 2), including satellites and airborne systems that destroyed the communication between Iraqi fighters and surface-to-air missile (Mann, 1994). The U.S. military used C^4I—which stands for command, control, communications, computer, and intelligence—to gather intelligence, make decision, and communicate such decisions to the field units.

A decade after the conclusion of the First Gulf War, the U.S. launched another attack in the Middle East. The War on Terror was waged to retaliate against the 9/11 attack. The U.S. claimed that Afghanistan and Iraq had weapons of mass destruction even though they were never found. Two suspects who master-minded the 9/11 attack—Saddam Hussein—former President of Iraq—and Osama Bin Laden—leader of Al-Qaeda—were killed. However, U.S. military actions also caused a large number of civilian casualties and created ongoing unrest in the region.

Because the War of Terror had no clearly identified enemies, the U.S. government had to create one: Muslims. Populations with Islamic faith living in the U.S. and abroad were targeted as potential terrorists who posed threats to national security. Massive misinformation campaigns were carried out to justify the necessity of War on Terror (Lean, n/a). In this case, information warfare is not only about using advanced communication technologies in the battleground but a holistic propaganda campaign carried out by governments, media, and advocacy groups (Lean, n/a). A report published by the Center for American Progress (Ali et al., 2011) suggested that misinformation about Muslims can be traced back to a small, tightly networked group who effectively spread Islamophobia through advocates, media partners, and grassroots organizing.

The War on Terror propaganda fed on Islamophobia. It aimed to stroke fears among populations in the West. The Bush Administration adhered to the narrative that Al-Qaeda orchestrated the 9/11 attack and "fanatical Muslims continue to constitute the major threat to the security of both Americans and the 'civilized' world" (Ralph, 2006, p. 278). The objects of fears are the Islam faith and Muslims. Islamophobia fosters "hostility toward Islam and Muslims that tends to dehumanize an entire faith, portraying it as fundamentally alien and attributing to it an inherent, essential set of negative traits such as irrationality, intolerance and violence" (Hollar & Naureckas, 2008, p. 4). Islamophobia systematically discriminates, marginalizes, and excludes Muslims from social, political, and civic life (Ali et al., 2011). Islamophobia asks citizens in the West to not only be wary of Middle Eastern countries, but also all Muslims regardless of their countries of origins, citizenship status, and political beliefs. As a result, incidents of harassment and discrimination experienced by American Muslims have exponentially increased since the War of Terror (Lean, n/a).

Lastly, this war has also compromised the civil liberty of U.S. citizens. The signing of USA Patriot Act into law gave domestic and federal law enforcement more power to monitor citizens' movements (Lean, n/a; Ralph, 2006). Most Americans are convinced that "terrorism" is such grave a problem that they are willing to trade promised security with "their taxes, their freedoms, their decimated public services, and their children's lives" (Ralph, 2006, p. 289). The War on Terror also endangered the democratic health of the nation when the freedom to religion was compromised (Ali et al., 2011). Even though the U.S. Constitution prohibits the government from making laws to ban practice of any religion, the discourse of War on Terror promoted Islam as a dangerous and deviant faith.

Misinformation has impacted western democratic institutions in a broader way. The election of Donald Trump in 2016 and the U.K. exit of the European Union (known as Brexit) are seen as paramount moments that show how misinformation could shape historical trajectory. Before running for the President, Donald Trump had questioned President Obama's citizen status (see Chapter 4, "Accessing", about the controversy). Trump's deeply racist attitude has publicly cracked open a Pandora's Box, legitimizing overt racism that is held by many in the country. The birther theory polarized the country, with some believing every American is equal while others believing white Americans should "take back" the country. This division has opened up opportunities for foreign powers, in this case Russia, to influence public opinion in the U.S.

Unlike the Cold War era during which foreign governments broadcast their messages through radio (such as Voice of America broadcast from West to East Germany), influencing public opinion in a foreign country is now done through social media such as Facebook and YouTube. In the next section, I will examine how highly specialized targeted ads on Facebook have provoked this social media giant to strengthen its monitoring of foreign governments' activities.

MISINFORMATION, DISINFORMATION, AND FAKE NEWS

Humans have spread false information—either intentionally and unintentionally—for a long time. An intentional case is military disseminating false information to enemies with the hope of misleading them. An example of an unintentional case is the belief that natural disasters were divine doings. Despite the long history of false information, the 2016 U.S. Presidential election had popularized concepts such as misinformation and fake news, making the public more aware that misinformation could quickly undo a democracy of several hundred years' standing.

Before diving into some incidents to show how false information could harm democracy, it is important to differentiate misinformation from disinformation. According to Wardle and Derakhshan (2018), misinformation is false information disseminated by a source who believes the information is true. In contrast, disinformation is false information disseminated by a source who knows that the information is false. While the difference is clear, readers usually have a hard time to decide if some false information is misinformation or disinformation because they cannot know the source's intention. Very often, readers may deduce a source's intention based on its perceived credibility. For example, quality newspapers such as *The New York Times* and *The Washington Post* are trusted to be credible news sources. However, President Trump has been branding news outlets as "fake news" whenever he does not agree with them. Readers who trust the President began to doubt the intention of news media and then dismissed their credibility.

The proliferation of social media also means that readers have a hard time to judge whether a source is credible or not. In fact, many social media users may be attracted to news on social media because this reinforces, not challenges, their views. The combination of dubious sources and highly selective news means social media users are susceptible to highly targeted political ads that reinforce political beliefs even if the ads have false information (Coppins, 2020). The election of Donald Trump as the 45th President of the United States is a case that shows the success of political ad targeting specific users on social media.

The winning of Trump was met with disbelief because most poll results showed his opponent Hillary Clinton leading with a comfortable margin. Political analysts explained that the polls may have overlooked potential voters who supported Trump while overcounting potential supporters of Clinton. One group that withdrew support from Clinton was African American voters who helped elect President Obama. Potential African American voters were targeted by hyper customized political ads. These ads were traced to trolls who were hired by the Russian government to interfere the U.S. election. Russian officials believed a Clinton presidency would pose difficulties to U.S.–Russia relations so they launched campaigns to elect Trump who was believed to be more friendly with the Russian government. Russian operatives targeted potential African American voters by showing them disinformation ads and social media posts. These ads and posts mimicked social justice campaigns that expose the racist attitudes of white politicians and law enforcement. The campaign confused the users by appropriating the hashtag #Blacklivesmatter as #BlackMatters. In addition, the campaign gave false information about how to vote, they told potential voters that they could cast their votes by texting ("Russian trolls' chief target", 2019). While the short-term goal of the Russian government was to elect Trump, a larger goal was to create political dissonances that undermine democracy in the U.S. (Swaine, 2018).

After the 2016 Presidential election, Facebook has strengthened its policies on political ads. To safeguard democratic social media campaigns for the 2020 election, Facebook vowed to combat inauthentic behaviour by taking down sites with fake accounts, provide more information about the page owners, explicate content that comes from partially or wholly state-owned, and decrease distribution of misinformation, and remove false information and threats about voting ("Helping to protect the 2020 US elections", n/a). Facebook also changed its advertising policies by stopping all political ads a week before and indefinitely after the 2020 election to "'reduce opportunities for confusion or abuse'" (Paul, 2020, para. 4).

In 2019, Facebook and Twitter have shown their quick actions to stop misinformation distribution. In 2019, pro-democracy protestors in Hong Kong, a semi-autonomous region of China, took to the streets to demand for more democracy and self-governing autonomy. One of the demands was to lay out a process to elect the city chief executive as promised in the Joint Sino–British Declaration signed in 1984. Hong Kong protestors appealed to the international community (such as the U.N.) and foreign governments (such as the U.S. and U.K.) for support. To counter the protestors, the Chinese government created fake accounts and posted misinformation that aimed to undermine the democracy protests in Hong Kong. They were hoping that misinformation would sway the public in the international community to think about Hong Kong protesters as rioters. Facebook and Twitter were quick to spot that these posts were coordinated by a Chinese state-backed agency (Lee, 2019) and soon removed the unverified accounts.

In this section, I suggest that misinformation has long been used in human communication. Sometimes false information is spread intentionally, sometimes not. The 2016 U.S. election popularized the use of "misinformation" and "fake news" in daily lives. By denouncing U.S. mainstream media producing "fake news", Trump has opened up an opportunity for a foreign government to directly influence public opinion in the U.S. by spreading real fake news. Nevertheless, the heightened awareness of misinformation ads on social media also led companies to take actions and made users more vigilant.

BIG DATA: BENEFITS FOR CONSUMERS?

In the previous sections, I have shown how governments control the populations through collecting and using information. I argue that by using a critical lens, the questions that we ask about information are more than about privacy. We seek an understanding of how information collection and application have social implications. Moreover, a critical lens looks beyond information equity, but uses gender and race as vantage points from where to critique how organizations use power to shape gender and race relations.

In this section, I shift the focus from governments to corporations. I want to understand how Big Data are used by corporations to control consumers' wants and needs. According to Harvey (2005), corporations have been using information technologies to accumulate, store, transfer, analyze, and use massive databases to guide decisions in the global marketplace. In the following, I will first review how businesses define Big Data, then I will summarize what solutions Big Data are said to provide for different industries, and finally I will examine how large corporations—such as Amazon and Netflix—use Big Data to control their customers.

Big Data has drawn attention among computing companies and analysts in the early 2000s when data became too fast, complex, and large to be processed by using traditional methods ("Big Data: What it is", n/a). Gartner, a research and advisory company that helps executives make decisions, defined big data as "high-volume, high-velocity and/or high-variety information assets that demand cost-effective, innovative forms of information processing that enable enhanced insight, decision making, and process automation" ("Big Data", n/a). Oracle, a company that provides cloud applications and infrastructure for companies and governments, stated that three Vs define Big Data: volume, velocity, and variety.

First, Big Data deals with a voluminous amount of unstructured data that may have unknown value. For example, data feeds on social media. The amount of data are measured at tens of terabytes. Second, Big Data travels in high velocity: it is quickly generated and received; it requires speedy actions, very often real-time evaluation and actions. Third, Big Data has great variety; they can be unstructured and semi-structured (such as text, audio, and video); some data requires further processing for analysts from which to derive meanings "What is Big Data", n/a). The forms and sources of data vary, they may come from sensors, devices, the internet, and social media generated through artificial intelligence (AI), mobile technologies, social media, and the Internet of Things ("Big Data analytics", n/a).

According to Oracle, Big Data are not mere numbers, they have intrinsic value. However, this value needs to be "discovered" by analysts, business users and executives when they ask the right questions, recognize patterns, make informed assumptions, and predict behaviors. For example, Amazon generates a lot of data, but the company needs to hire analysts to understand them ("What is Big Data", n/a). Analysis of Big Data would help firm increase profits because they reduce cost and time, help develop new products, and assist making smart decisions ("Big Data: What it is", n/a).

Big Data are supposed to find its applications in a range of industries: from retail to manufacturing, education to government, banking to healthcare. For example, Big Data can provide insights for retailers to predict trends, forecast consumers' demands, optimize prices, identify potential customers and decide how to best market products to them. Retailers may use Big Data tools to crawl social media posts and web browsing habits to see what the next trends are. They can also adjust prices by tracking consumers' demand, inventory levels, and competitor activities (Marr, 2015).

Executives in healthcare industry can also use Big Data. Dash, Shakyawar, Sharma, and Kaushik (2019) suggested that a data repository that collects data from different sources will aid smarter and cost-effective healthcare decisions because healthcare providers can quickly review patients' data and identify specialized medicine. Big Data for better healthcare will combine records of healthcare providers, insurance companies, pharmacists; results of genomics-driven experiments; and data from sensors from Internet-enabled smart devices.

The education sector can also use Big Data. Techniques such as data mining, data analytics, and web dashboards may eliminate some drudgery of routine testing and learning assessment (West, 2012). Instead of using a one-size-fits-all periodic testing, data provide teachers insights into what the students already know and what techniques are the most effective for students with varying preparedness. Data mining techniques can draw in metrics such as academic perspective, disciplinary problems, and attendance to predict which students are likely to drop out of school. Lastly, web dashboards can visually display metrics for school administrators to monitor learning, performance, and behavioral issues.

While Big Data may bring better healthcare and education experience, the technologies are costly to hospitals and schools. However, hi-tech companies that have plenty of resources are already harnessing the power of Big Data in the name of serving consumers better. In the following, I will show that the power of these companies may reduce consumers' choices and eliminate competitors.

Netflix and Amazon are two technology companies that collect voluminous data of customers. The data that they collect are proprietary, they are not available for their competitors or the public to use. The reason why these data are proprietary is because they provide insights into consumers' behaviors, which assist the companies to make business decisions. Even though Netflix and Amazon are in the businesses of online streaming and retailing, what makes the two companies high-value is the amount of Big Data that they have and the algorithm that they use to process these data. The power of these two companies not only drives away smaller competitors, but it also coerces other companies—big or small—to agree to their terms. When companies like Netflix and Amazon control most of the markets, consumers are left with few real choices.

Netflix began as a mailing DVD rental company and later became an online streaming company when broadband Internet allowed for faster data transmission. Unlike movie theaters, network and cable television channels, Netflix appears to offer more choices to the viewers for they can choose what, when, and where to watch. However, it is also questionable whether Netflix provides the viewers with more freedom to consume media or curates for them a specific media experience. Netflix is able to do this because they use Big Data to recommend personalized choices and to produce data-driven new content.

Big Data is a prime strategy employed by Netflix (Fernández-Manzano, Neira, & Clares-Gavilán, 2016). They argue that Netflix's first business objective is to retain customers and avoid cancellation. To achieve this objective, they need to know consumers' preferences, habits and behaviors by collecting data such as profile information, ratings and comments In addition, they collect data generated during viewing, such as viewed or discarded content type, viewing speed, re-watch, frequency and amount of time of watching, and the devices on which the content is consumed. Both kinds of data provide Netflix with insights into why and how viewers watch certain content.

After analyzing viewers' habits, Netflix uses algorithm to make recommendations to viewers. This process is not yet fully-automated. They hire human "taggers" to watch shows, categorize content and assign tags. They create 80,000 microgenres in the Netflix catalogue (Fernández-Manzano, Neira, & Clares-Gavilán, 2016) that allow Netflix make "top picks" recommendations for viewers. Some of the recommendations are popular titles, others are titles with a limited cycle (such as holiday films). Netflix also remembers where viewers halt their watching and would remind them what they left off.

Big Data not only helps Netflix understand the consumers better, but they also help the company decide what shows to make. When Netflix branched out into media production and decided to make *House of Cards*, it raised eyebrows among television producers. Netflix defied a few industry standards such as making pilots, conducting focus groups, previewing shows to advertisers, and releasing one episode at a time. Netflix was able to break all rules because it relied on Big Data to understand consumers' habits. They understand which types of show consumers like, and they understand how viewers watch TV shows (Smith & Telang, 2016).

Amazon is another company that collects users' information and analyzes it for the company's own advantage. Amazon began as an online bookseller and then became an online shopping mall with all types of merchandise. It also does media production and provides cloud services. Unlike bricks-and-mortar retailers that first receive shipment from wholesalers and wait for sales to understand market demand, Amazon can quickly determine market demand by analyzing data generated from web browsing and online purchases. Also unlike bricks-and-mortar retailers that may need to do in-person trips to check the price points of their competitors, Amazon can mine data from online retailers for price comparison. These data allow Amazon to do "dynamic pricing", which is frequently changing the prices to respond to market demand ("How Amazon used Big Data to rule e-commerce", 2019). On average, the cost of every product changes every ten minutes (Mehta, Detroja, & Agashe, 2018). Some users have discovered that if they look at the same products during the course of a day, the price for that item may keep on going up.

Does Amazon offer customers more choices? While it is true that consumers could just go to this one site for all shopping needs, Amazon also knows how to manipulate prices to make profits. For example, it offers a more competitive prices on some common items, but the prices for other goods are not as competitive. The competitive prices on select items give consumers an illusion that Amazon offers the best price throughout. In addition, Amazon analyzes patterns of customers' behaviors and recommends them to buy more than they need (Mehta, Detroja, & Agashe, 2018). (Interestingly, it actually asked consumers to not overbuy during the COVID-19 pandemics because its workers cannot meet the surging demands overnight.) Lastly, Amazon collects a wide range of consumers' data through its handheld devices and artificial intelligence assistant, online streaming and cloud storage. When Amazon Prime members use their online identity to check in different Amazon services, the company simultaneously learn a lot about consumers' behaviors. For example, if a user asks an artificial intelligence assistant to look up a technical term, Amazon.com can recommend books that are about such subject matters. In another example, if a user shops for grocery, Amazon.com can then suggest to this user what kitchen gadgets can be purchased to prepare the ingredients.

Despite the power that Netflix and Amazon have over consumers, some are convinced that they are informed consumers who are not influenced by these companies. While it is true that consumers have some autonomy to choose what items to consume and where to buy them, they cannot control how Netflix and Amazon drive out competitors, especially the smaller ones. The elimination of competitors will eventually harm consumers because they will have less choice in the market.

The story of Netflix driving video rental company Blockbuster out of business has been used as a cautionary tale of creative destruction and disruptive innovation. Blockbuster was once the leading video rental company in the U.S. with 9,000 stores in the country. Netflix once offered itself to be acquired by Blockbuster but was rejected. Blockbuster did not foresee that online streaming would one day take over rental; it also could not predict the power of data in the business of entertainment. The decline of rental stores is often said to be a case study of creative destruction—the tendency of old mode of capitalist production being destructed in order to create a new economic order (Schumpeter, 2010)—and disruptive innovation—the ability of small businesses to challenge established businesses by tapping into an underserved consumer segment (Christensen, Raynor, & McDonald, 2015). However, Netflix also drove a lot of mom-and-pop video rental shops out of business. These shops, especially those in small towns and rural areas, serve as community places for viewers who may not have broadband Internet at home and for those who want to browse a huge variety of titles (Phillips, 2015).

Similar to Netflix, Amazon drives out mall online retailers by offering free and fast shipping to its members. Small businesses are left with few options. They could follow the lead of Amazon and offer free and fast shipping or they could partner with Amazon to sell their ware on its site. There are many cases to show how Amazon exploits these partners. For example, Amazon forced the publisher Hachette to offer a deep discount for new titles. When the publisher refused to do so, Amazon retaliated by delaying shipments of their titles and failing to show their books on search (Kellogg, 2014). In another example, Amazon closely watches the sale of products; once some products become popular, it undercuts small businesses by directly sourcing products from the wholesalers, offering a cheaper price to compete with these small businesses, and making their products harder to find (Merrill, 2014).

How do the lenses of gender and race inform the use of Big Data and the power of corporations? On the one hand, Netflix and Amazon may appear to empower women and minorities because they give them more choices and offer them online convenience. For example, Netflix recommends genres that cater to women and minority groups, Amazon allows people of color to browse online without worrying being followed around by shop assistants. Both places allow women more flexibility in juggling their duties. However, corporations only care about women and minorities when they are consumers, they do not care about them as citizens. According to Gandy (1993), Big Data is used to sort individuals according to presumed economic value, such as the types of consumers they are perceived. It precisely classifies individuals according to their perceived value in the marketplace.

Amazon offers an excellent example to show how a corporation can use its power to not only control consumers and small businesses, but also government. The market value of Amazon—estimated to be US$1 trillion—comes from data provided by consumers and mined from the Internet. However, it is a known secret that despite the profits, Amazon had not always paid corporate taxes to the federal government. Therefore, the money that it makes does not contribute to public goods, such as roads and airports that are necessary for Amazon packages to be delivered. It also does not contribute to public services such as education that trains the next generation of Amazon workforce. In addition to not contributing to public goods, Amazon also demands local governments to maximize the corporation's profits in the name of benefiting local residents. When Amazon announced that it sought proposals from U.S. cities to build the second headquarters, the company attracted more than 200 proposals. Like contestants in a beauty contest, cities displayed their strengths such as infrastructure, affordable living cost, and an educated workforce. Cities also promised to provide generous tax cuts and boost local spending. For those that did not make the cuts, Amazon voluntarily told city governments areas to improve even though the company never ran a city.

Eventually Amazon chose New York City to be the winner. Rather than celebrating to be the chosen one, New Yorkers and local politicians cited concerns that Amazon jobs would not bring benefits to all populations. Amazon jobs would attract highly educated employees who will move to the city and drive up property prices. This will make service workers—mostly consist of immigrants and women of color—having a harder time to find decent housing in the city (Newton, 2019). Even though some may think it was a wrong decision for the city to decline the offer, it was at least a small victory of the working-class populations in one of the most expensive cities in the world.

CONCLUSION

Organizations, such as governments and corporations, have more power to use information than individuals. Even though governments could use information to benefit the public, it also uses information to control the population. I began by showing how the U.S. census has selectively omitted certain populations by not recognizing them as citizens. How the U.S. census named non-white groups also had implications for recognizing differentiated experiences in society. Even though in recent years the U.S. census has become more inclusive, the "check box" approach to race still renders certain groups, such as populations self-identify as Middle Eastern or North African, invisible. In addition, white is still the dominant race because it is listed as the first choice.

Some governments aim to serve the populations better by issuing national identity cards that link taxation and health information to social benefits. Populations in democratic nations believe national identity cards are surveillance tools that violate civil liberty. Those in non-democratic nations have little choice but to accept them. They are also subject to additional surveillance when states use facial recognition technology and closed-circuit television to track citizens' movements.

Information is also imperative to modern warfare. The First Gulf War was dubbed the first information war because U.S. military used advanced technologies to intercept communication of the enemies. However, information in warfare may also mean something more encompassing, such as information campaigns to create fear among populations. The War on Terror that the U.S. waged against a faceless enemy used Islamophobia to convince citizens why invading Afghanistan and Iraq could keep Americans safe. The ramifications are long-lasting on Muslims living in both the U.S. and abroad. Muslim men, in particular, have been harassed and stigmatized as potential terrorists. Even though misinformation has been disseminated to demonize Muslims and the Islamic faith, the 2016 Presidential election in U.S. popularized the concept misinformation. The election showed foreign governments could use social media to sway political opinions of potential voters. The Russian government sought to divide the U.S. populations and undermine democracy by persuading African American voters to not participate in the election.

The last section looks at how corporations use Big Data to maximize profits. While Big Data are promised to aid better decision-making for a wide range of industries, resourceful corporations can harness the power of Big Data better than impoverished school districts or local governments. Netflix and Amazon are two corporations that use Big Data to attract and retain customers. Even though both promise to offer an array of choices, they also limit consumers' choices by making recommendations based on previous purchases and other consumers' choices. In addition, both corporations drive away small businesses that are not equipped with Big Data technology. I also argue at the end of the chapter that Amazon also exercises its power over governments, exempting itself from paying corporate taxes while reaping benefits from local governments.

BIBLIOGRAPHY

1790 overview. (n/a). United States Census Bureau. Retrieved from: https://www.census.gov/history/www/through_the_decades/overview/1790.html

1850. (n/a). United States Census Bureau. Retrieved from: https://www.census.gov/history/www/through_the_decades/questionnaires/1850_2.html

Ali, W., Clifton, E., Duss, M., Fang, L., Keyes, S., & Shakir, F. (2011). *Fear, Inc.: The roots of the islamophobia network in America*. Washington, DC: Center for American Progress.

Aoki, M. (2016, August 23). Government to loosen rules on using maiden names for My Number, residence cards. *The Japan Times*. Retrieved from: https://www.japantimes.co.jp/

Big Data. Gartner. Retrieved from: https://www.gartner.com/en/information-technology/glossary/big-data

Big data analytics. IBM. Retrieved from: https://www.ibm.com/analytics/hadoop/big-data-analytics

Big Data: What it is and why it matters. SAS. Retrieved from: https://www.sas.com/en_us/insights/big-data/what-is-big-data.html

Braman, S. (2006). *Change of state: Information, policy, and power*. Cambridge, MA: MIT Press.

Brown, A. (2020, February 25). The changing categories the U.S. Census has used to measure race. *Pew Research Center*. Retrieved from: https://www.pewresearch.org/fact-tank/2020/02/25/the-changing-categories-the-u-s-has-used-to-measure-race/

Bureau of the Census. (1921). *Population 1920: Number and distribution of inhabitants*. Washington, DC: Government Printing Office.

Chen, S. (2017, October 17). China to build giant facial reconnection database to identify any citizen within seconds. *South China Morning Post*. Retrieved from: https://www.scmp.com

Christensen, C. M., Raynor, M. E., & McDonald, R. (2015, December). What is disruptive innovation? *Harvard Business Review*. Retrieved from: https://hbr.org/2015/12/what-is-disruptive-innovation

Coppins, M. (2020, March). The 2020 disinformation war. *Atlantic Monthly*, pp. 30–39.

Dash, S., Shakyawar, S. K., Sharma, M., & Kaushik, S. (2019). Big data in healthcare: Management, analysis and future prospects. *Journal of Big Data*, 6(54). Retrieved from: https://doi.org/10.1186/s40537-019-0217-0

Fernández-Manzano, E-P., Neira, E., & Clares-Gavilán, J. (2016). Data management in audiovisual business: *Netflix* as a case study. *El Profesional de la Información, 25*(4), 568–576.

Gandy, O. H. (1993). *The panoptic sort: A political economy of personal information.* Boulder, CO: Westview.

Gupta, S. (2020, March 8). To fight discrimination, the U.S. Census needs a different race question. *Science News*. Retrieved from: https://www.sciencenews.org/article/census-2020-race-ethnicity-questions

Harvey, D. (2005). *A brief history of neoliberalism.* Oxford: Oxford University Press.

Helping to protect the 2020 US elections. Facebook. Retrieved from: https://about.fb.com/news/2019/10/update-on-election-integrity-efforts/

Hollar, J., & Naureckas, J. (2008, October). *Smearcasting: How Islamophobes spread fear, bigotry and misinformation.* New York: Fairness and Accuracy in Reporting.

How Amazon used Big Data to rule e-commerce. (2019, November 30). *Inside Big Data*. Retrieved from: https://insidebigdata.com/2019/11/30/how-amazon-used-big-data-to-rule-e-commerce/

ID system raises thorny issues. (2013, March 30). *Japan Times*. Retrieved from: https://www.japantimes.co.jp/opinion/2013/03/30/editorials/id-system-raises-thorny-issues/#.XpkGl257mS8

Kellogg, C. (2014, June 3). Amazon and Hachette: The dispute in 13 easy steps. *The Los Angeles Times*. Retrieved from: https://www.latimes.com/books/jacketcopy/la-et-jc-amazon-and-hachette-explained-20140602-story.html

Kennedy, J. C. G. (1864). *Population of the United States in 1860: Compiled from the original returns of the Eighth Census.* Washington, DC: Government Printing Office.

Lean, N. (n/a). Islamophobia in the United States: A case of the three "I"s. *Oxford Islamic Studies Online*. Retrieved from: http://www.oxfordislamicstudies.com/Public/focus/essay1009_islamophobia_united_states.html

Lee, D. (2019, August 20). Hong Kong protests: Twitter and Facebook remove Chinese accounts. *BBC*. Retrieved from: https://www.bbc.com/news/technology-49402222

Mann, E. (1994). Desert storm: The first information war? *Aerospace Power Journal*. Retrieved from: http://www.iwar.org.uk/iwar/resources/airchronicles/man1.htm

Marr, B. (2015, November 10). Big Data: A game changer in the retail sector. *Forbes*. Retrieved from: https://www.forbes.com/sites/bernardmarr/2015/11/10/big-data-a-game-changer-in-the-retail-sector/#5e60c2499f37

Mathieson, SA. (2018, June 19). National ID cards might not mean much when up against incompetence of the UK Home Office. *The Register*. Retrieved from: https:/www.theregister.co.uk

McCarthy, A. (2015, August 4). Calais and the UK's lack of ID cards. *BBC*. Retrieved from https://www.bbc.com

McGinty, J. C. (2020, July 25–26). Documenting race proves tricky for census. *Wall Street Journal*, p. A2.

McGlinn, L. A. (1991). Early Chinese immigrants and the United States Census. *American Association of Geographers Middle States Division, 24*, 113–120.

Mehta, N., Detroja, P., & Agashe, A. (2018, August 10). Amazon changes prices on its products about every 10 minutes: Here's how and why they do it. *Business Insider*. Retrieved from: https://www.businessinsider.com/amazon-price-changes-2018-8

Merrill, J. (2014, September 5). Amazon under fire for "bullying and exploiting small retailers". *The Independent*. Retrieved from: https://www.independent.co.uk/news/business/news/amazon-under-fire-for-bullying-and-exploiting-small-retailers-9715502.html

NALEO Educational Fund. (2019, December). *Policy brief: The Hispanic origin and race questions in census 2020: Making the best of missed opportunities and a flawed approach.* Retrieved from: https://hagasecontar.org/wp-content/uploads/2019/12/The-Hispanic-Origin-and-Race-Questions-in-Census-2020-Final.pdf

Newton, C. (2019, February 15). What Amazon got wrong about New York City. *The Verge*. Retrieved from: https://www.theverge.com/interface/2019/2/15/18225646/amazon-nyc-hq2-collapse-secrecy-incentives-automation

Osaki, T. (2015). Plaintiffs across Japan charge that My Number ID system is unconstitutional. *The Japan Times*. Retrieved from: https://www.japantimes.co.jp/

Paul, K. (2020, October 7). Facebook announces plan to stop political ads after 3 November. *The Guardian*. Retrieved from: https://www.theguardian.com/technology/2020/oct/07/facebook-stop-political-ads-policy-3-november

Philbrick, S. (2018, September 16). Understanding the three-fifths compromise. *Constitutional Accountability Center*. Retrieved from: https://www.theusconstitution.org/news/understanding-the-three-fifths-compromise/

Phillips, C. (2015, January 9). The "rent" stuff: Small town, mom-and-pop stores are a vestige of video rental heyday. *Chattanooga Times Free Press*. Retrieved from: https://www.timesfreepress.com/news/life/entertainment/story/2015/jan/09/rent-stuffsmall-town-mom-and-pop-stores-are-v/281511/

Ralph, D. (2006). Islamophobia and the "war on terror": The continuing pretext for U.S. imperial conquest. *Research in Political Economy, 23*, 261–298.

Roberts, K., & Webster, F. (1988). Cybernetic capitalism: Information, technology, everyday life. In V. Mosco & J. Wasko (Eds.), *The political economy of information* (pp. 44–75). Madison, WI: The University of Wisconsin Press.

Runes, C. (2019, February 26). Following a long history, the 2020 Census risks undercounting the black population. *Urban Wire*. Retrieved from: https://www.urban.org/urban-wire/following-long-history-2020-census-risks-undercounting-black-population

Russian trolls' chief target was 'black US voters' in 2016. (2019, October 9). *BBC*. Retrieved from: https://www.bbc.com/news/technology-49987657

Schumpeter, J. A. (2010). *Capitalism, socialism, and democracy*. New York: Routledge.

Smith, M. D., & Telang, R. (2016). *Streaming, sharing, stealing: Big data and the future of entertainment*. Cambridge, MA: MIT Press

Swaine, J. (2018, December 17). Russian propagandists targeted African Americans to influence 2016 US election. *The Guardian*. Retrieved from: https://www.

theguardian.com/us-news/2018/dec/17/russian-propagandists-targeted-african-americans-2016-election

Tao, L. (2018, January 23). A look at China's push for digital national ID cards. *South China Morning Post*. Retrieved from: https://www.scmp.com/tech/article/2129957/look-chinas-push-national-digital-id-cards

Timeline: ID cards. (2010, May 27). *BBC*. Retrieved from: https://www.bbc.com/news/10164331

Totenberg, N., & Wang, H. L. (2019, June 27). Trump threatens census delay after Supreme Court leaves citizenship question blocked. *WBUR*. Retrieved from: https://www.wbur.org/npr/717635291/supreme-court-leaves-citizenship-question-blocked-from-2020-census

Travis, A. (2010, May 27). ID cards scheme to be scrapped within 100 days. *The Guardian*. Retrieved from http://www.theguardian.com

Valid concerns over My Number. (2015, October 2). *Japan Times*. Retrieved from https://www.japantimes.co.jp/

Van Boom, D. (2020, January 22). Chinese city uses surveillance tech to shame citizens for wearing pyjamas outside. *CNET*. Retrieved from http://www.cnet.com

Waddell, K. (2016, April 8). How big data harms poor communities. *The Atlantic*. Retrieved from: https://www.theatlantic.com/technology/archive/2016/04/how-big-data-harms-poor-communities/477423/

Walker, F. A. (1872). *The statistics of the population of the United States*. Washington, DC: Government Printing Office.

Wang, H. L. (2019, March 31). What you need to know about the 2020 census. *WBUR News*. Retrieved from: https://www.wbur.org/npr/707899218/what-you-need-to-know-about-the-2020-census

Wardle, C., & Derakhshan, H. (2018). Thinking about "information disorder": Formats of misinformation, disinformation, and mal-information. In C. Ireton & J. Posetti (Eds.), *Journalism, "fake news" and disinformation* (pp. 43–54). UNESCO.

West, D. M. (2012, September). Big Data for education: Data mining, data analytics, and web dashboards. Washington, DC: Brookings Institution.

What is Big Data? Oracle. Retrieved from: https://www.oracle.com/big-data/what-is-big-data.html

Wright, C. D. (1900). *The history and growth of the United States census*. Washington, DC: Government Printing Office.

6

CREATING

INTRODUCTION

It was once possible to read all the books in the Library of Congress. In 1812, the library held 3,076 volumes. If a man of leisure—for women were less likely to be literate or to have the time—had read one book a day, it would have taken him less than nine years to do so. Nowadays, no person could possibly read the 25 million books in the Library of Congress ("General information", n/a). Even at a rate of reading one book per day, it would take a fast reader 68,500 years to complete the task. And it would be hard to keep up because the library adds 10,000 items to the collection every working day ("Fascinating facts", n/a). And book is only one source of information; there are also other print (such as newspapers and magazines), audiovisual (such as television, radio, and film) and online materials.

The exponential growth of information in the past 200 years not only illustrates that the average person consumes more information, but it also illustrates that the average person *creates* more information by using a wider variety of technologies. How can we explain the increase in the amount of information produced? One reason is the sevenfold increase in the world population from 1820s to 2020.

Another reason is the rise of literacy rate. In this chapter, we focus on a third reason: the invention of digital technologies that allows faster and easier ways to create and share information.

Digital technologies have significantly lowered the cost and shortened the time to produce and distribute information. In an analogue age, information creators needed specific and expensive equipment to produce their work; very often the specialty was so niche that every part of the job required a specialist. For example, journalists would type up their stories with a typewriter, typesetters would prepare the printing block, printers would duplicate the copies. Nowadays, journalists often write up their pieces on a computer, shoot their own videos on a cell phone, and upload them online.

Professionals are not the only ones who benefit from digital technologies, amateurs benefit as well. Digital devices, such as the cell phone, are getting cheaper; they have multiple functions and are easy to use. Digital technologies have definitely enabled more people to become creators, making diverse viewpoints known and enriching a marketplace of ideas. It is therefore not a wonder why the Library of Congress has to keep on acquiring materials even though no one single person can possibly read all the books!

However, the abundance of information does not mean information production and distribution is democratic. New information and communication technologies (ICT) companies have tremendous power to decide how and what information should be produced and distributed. It wields power by providing technologies that on the surface allow users to produce a wide range of information, but the distribution and consumption of this information is often controlled by the same companies. Take the Apple iPhone as an example. The company advertises to amateurs that its professional grade camera could take breathtaking pictures. However, the digital pictures have to go through other Apple software (such as iPhoto) and platforms (such as iCloud) for distribution and consumption. This is unlike photography where the manufacturers of the camera cannot control the film brand and the printing service that photographers use. This false sense of new freedom in turn masks the power relation between ICT companies and consumers; consumers are asked to thank these companies for offering them new freedom to create!

ICT companies heavily promote to users their freedom to create information. This shows that information has value, but can we measure the value of information? If amateur-created information does have value for ICT companies, then how does the process work? If everyone can create information, what sets professionals apart from amateurs? Lastly, is there a way to create information without being controlled by ICT companies?

What is the Value of Information?

In this chapter, I will first contrast two theoretical standpoints that differ in seeing the value of information: neoclassical economics and a political economy of communication. The two standpoints differ in how they conceptualize the relation between social actors in a market. Neoclassical economists believe that the market produces information (Babe, 1995, 1996) which signals to producers what are in demand. In contrast, political economists believe that information, along with digital technologies, are commodities produced for and in a market. Using amateur information producers as an example, neoclassical economists would argue that if certain information is in demand—such as DIY content produced by an "average person"—then the market needs to supply more similar goods for consumers. Political economists, on the other hand, would argue that the market of DIY content is created by powerful companies. Amateur producers, despite appear to be successful self-employed entrepreneurs, self-exploit their labor. The ones who benefit the most by DIY content are these powerful ICT companies.

What is the Commodification of Information?

Political economists would argue that the commodification of information would explain why there is such an explosion of information in the digital age. Information, like tangible goods such as cars and food, is a commodity bought and sold in a market. However, unlike tangible goods, commodified information blurs the boundary between producers and consumers. For example, automobile workers get paid for producing cars, but users do not get paid for generating content for social media. In addition, social media users have to watch ads before accessing the supposedly "free" information generated by themselves and others. Another way to think about the commodification of information is intellectual property (Garnham, 1979). While stealing someone's car is a punishable crime, is duplicating digital content a punishable crime as well? For the former, the car owner loses a tangible goods; for the latter, the content remains the same. Political economists argue that information companies see information, like cars, as a private property. This private property, however, does not belong to individuals such as the engineers who invent the technologies. This private property belongs to companies such as Amazon or Google. Finally, I ask why some information remains expensive to the public despite the explosive amount of information. For example, even though any literate person with reliable Internet connection can read ebooks from the public library, the cost of higher education keeps going up.

Who Are Information Producers?

Information creators nowadays do not have to be employed by a media organization, there are amateur and self-employed media producers. In addition, the media organization is not the only kind of organization that employs information workers: banks, educational institutions, manufacturing, and medicine also employ information workers. In fact, most professions would require some interactions with information: some require years of training (such as software programming), some only need days (such as retailing). If most professions in most industries ask workers to interact with information, does it mean everyone is an information worker? The definition of information workers has become so fuzzy that it warrants some attention.

Resisting Information Commodification

In the face of commodified information, activists and artists have proposed alternative ways to share knowledge. They believe that we must stand on the shoulders of giants to advance knowledge for public goods (Benkler, 2006). Human knowledge will stagnate if information is privatized and commodified by powerful companies. When information is seen as a private property, others are not able to build on it.

To counter privatized information, some activists work on alternative forms of intellectual property, such as "copyleft" and knowledge commons; others provoke discussion by critiquing privatized information. Even though we may all feel powerless to counter powerful companies, it does not mean we do not have any power. Allocating information as a public resource is a way to resist such hegemony.

WHAT IS THE VALUE OF INFORMATION?

Does information have value? Does it have *a* value? (Babe, 1995; Bates, 1988).

The first question is about the use value of information: Is information valuable to you? The second question is about exchange value: How much will you pay for information (Fuchs & Mosco, 2012; Gandy, 1993; Jhally & Livant, 1986)?

Consider the value of this book. If a reader considers this book to be valuable, it means the information serves some purposes, such as completing an assignment or learning new knowledge. If a reader considers a book a good buy, it means the cost justifies the use value. The former value—use value—cannot be quantified while the latter one—exchange value—can be quantified.

According to Marx (1999), use value of goods fulfills human needs, such as hunger and thirst; exchange value of a goods is the price that someone is willing to pay for a goods in a market (Harvey, 1982). While the distinction between use value and exchange value may be straightforward, it is not always the case. The first reason is that use value may be perceived differently from one person to the next (Harvey, 1982). To give an example, all humans need to fulfill the need to eat and drink. If one is left with $10 in one's pocket, one may prioritize food because it fulfills a basic human need. However, if one has $1 billion in one's pocket, then one may expand the list of goods that can fulfill basic needs, such as a big house, an expensive car or some luxury items such as a diamond ring. In the case of the billionaire, basic needs may include satisfying hunger and thirst as well as a display of wealth.

The second reason why the distinction between use value and exchange value is not always that clear cut is because exchange value could be used to determine use value rather than use value determining exchange value. For example, food sustains life but the same kind of food comes with different prices: national brand costs more than store brand; organic food costs more than non-organic food. Consumers sometimes are willing to believe that food with a higher price tag has better quality and comes with more nutrients. The perception that more expensive food is better means that exchange value determines use value. Sometimes, exchange value creates use value. For example, stores promote deep discounts luring consumers to believe that we need goods that we actually don't. In this case, the discounted price (exchange value) leads us to believe the goods have use value.

In addition to the difficulty to distinguish use value from exchange value, another complication is the difference between tangible goods and intangible goods. Tangible goods are goods that we can touch and see and they are exhaustible. For example, we can touch food and cars. When a car dealer sells a car, he/she will have one fewer cars to sell. In contrast, intangible goods are goods that we cannot touch and see, and they are usually inexhaustible (Lessig, 2001). For example, information is intangible goods, the quantity and quality remain the same even after it is used once (Bates, 1988). For example, after a file is downloaded, it can be downloaded an infinite number of times.

Since information comprises inexhaustible goods, therefore the exchange value should be very low, if not free (Gandy, 1993). However, this is clearly not the case. Why is it the case that some digital information (such as media goods, financial information and educational materials) is not only free, but very expensive? Neoclassical economists and political economists have different explanations about this high price tag. The different explanations reflect a fundamental difference between how neoclassical economists and political economists see information in the market.

Neoclassical economists believe that the market is a place where buyers and sellers meet. They assume both buyers and sellers have complete freedom to make informed choices in the market. In addition, they assume the market is an autonomous "thing" that is free of political control. When neoclassical economists see the market as an enclosed system, they believe market activities generate information such as consumer preference, market demand, and supply level (Babe, 1995; Harvey, 1982; Preda, 2009). All this information will aid decisions such as how much a goods should be priced. For example, if there is an increased demand of smartphones in the market, then manufacturers should increase supply to satisfy consumers' demand. If this demand cannot be met, manufacturers can increase smartphone price to make them less affordable. In another example, if there is an increased demand of DIY content produced by amateurs, then more similar content should be produced. While neoclassical economists have certainly offered some conventional wisdom about how to price a commodity, it does not explain why intangible goods can command a high price in the market.

Political economist Robert Babe (1995) pointed out a paradox of neoclassical economics: if the market generates information about market price, then how can it price the information that it generates? Political economists explain this paradox by seeing information as a commodity. To them, information, like tangible goods such as a smartphone, is a commodity that is bought and sold in the market. As a commodity, there is no intrinsic difference between information and a smartphone, both are produced for the market so that the sellers can make a profit. While this argument may not go against a neoclassical economic belief of how a market works, political economists point out one thing which neoclassical economists would disagree: the pricing of information is not generated by the market, but is set by companies. Therefore, the price of information can be completely arbitrary. If this is the case, then the market is not an autonomous "thing" that *only* registers the activities of buyers and sellers, but is controlled by a handful of information companies. These companies are so powerful that an unfree market actually benefits them. As I explained in Chapter 5, "Using", online retailer giant Amazon drives away small competitors and stifles competition. When the market is less free, the handful of powerful companies can set the price of information. Consumers have few options but to pay the price set by a handful of companies. To further delineate this argument about exchange value, it is important to trace back to history to review what Karl Marx (see Postone, 1993) said about the relation between labor, time, and value.

VALUE AND LABOR TIME

I explained earlier that Marx distinguished use value from exchange value; in this section I will summarize how he explained exchange value with labor time. Marx advanced a labor theory of value because value is calculated from the total labor time needed for the production of goods. He also offered a critique of value (Fuchs, 2011b). As suggested, he believed that use value fulfills human needs while exchange value is the market price of a piece of goods. As such, use value is concrete while exchange value is abstract (Harvey, 1982). For example, as a vegetarian, I prefer to satisfy my hunger with vegetables but a meat-lover would choose meat. The use value of food is thus relevant to individuals' preference. This need is concrete because I am the one who can tell whether I feel satisfied with the food that I eat or not (see Harvey, 2010).

In contrast, the exchange value of food is abstract. To consumers, regardless of their diet, they can compare the price of vegetable to that of meat. They can decide what to buy based on the amount of money that they have. Affluent consumers may be willing to exchange money with high quality food such as organic food and prime cut. Consumers with limited means have little choice. Even though money could evoke strong feelings, its purpose is very mundane. It is a medium of exchange and a yardstick for comparison. This mundane purpose of money illustrate that it is an objective measurement of exchange value.

The above example shows how use value and exchange value work for consumers. Use value and exchange value also apply to producers, such as farmers who grow the food and factory workers who make cars. In the case of most of the population, we make money by working. We work for those who have the capital to buy our time (Heydebrand, 2003). Some populations, however, may not need to work. Their money may come from other income sources such as investment dividends. To them, they do not exchange their time for money.

However, exchanging time for money is a recent phenomenon in human history. In the past, some worked to produce food and shelter to provide for themselves and their communities. These production has direct use value. They may sell their surplus goods in the market but the primary purpose of work was to provide goods with use value. Nowadays, we still produce goods with use value, but mostly during our spare time because capitalism has separated work from leisure (Roberts & Webster, 1988). For example, we pick up woodworking, sewing, or bread-making as hobbies. The time we spend on producing these useful goods is qualitative (Harvey, 1982): we tend not to measure the time we spend on production with the exchange value of goods that we produce. We tend to talk about how we enjoy the process of making useful things. Once we begin to calculate the exchange value of our time, we'd know it is much cheaper to buy the goods from the market.

To those of us who exchange our labor time with money, time is objective and measurable (see Harvey, 2010). For example, workers who have hourly-waged jobs are paid based on the time that they spend on the job. Hourly-waged jobs are often seen as dead-end jobs because workers will only make enough money to buy basic goods to sustain lives, they will not make enough money to open their own shops and be their own boss. To open one's own shop, workers will need to have the capital to pay for rent, inventory, and technologies; the wage for hourly jobs is set low, preventing workers from saving enough and becoming capitalists. Therefore, those who control the means of production, such as the technologies, also control the labor.

For those who control the means of production, such as shop owners, the question is then how they can price their goods so as to make a profit. In order to make a profit, the exchange value of goods should be more than the combined costs of labor time, raw materials, and overheads (Harvey, 2010). Because the costs for raw materials and overhead are relatively fixed, the only cost that owners can directly control is that of labor cost. In countries with no legal minimum wage, workers can easily be exploited. If the labor market is saturated with laborers, then capitalists can offer workers very low wages because of oversupply. In some cases, workers' wages are so low that the money they make by selling their labor time is not sufficient for them to sustain lives, less of buying the goods that their labor produces. Throughout history, there are also many cases where the labor cost was kept low. Slavery is an example of how owners reap the profits of others' labor power without paying for their time. Child labor and prison labor are yet other examples to show how the "idle" time of some are turned into a profit for others.

I have so far shown the relationship between labor time and exchange value. The above examples, however, only focus on tangible goods, such as food and cars. This relationship becomes more complicated when the goods is intangible and inexhaustible, such as information (Babe, 1995). As suggested, information is intangible because we cannot see or touch it; it is also inexhaustible because its quality and quantity remain the same no matter how many times people buy it. In addition to these two peculiar characteristics of intangible goods, there are three specific ones to information. First, the use value of information is not universal (Babe, 1996). Some information, such as weather forecasts, may be useful for some but others only have use value to a select few. For example, medical information written in highly technical language will not be useful to those who are not trained in medicine. Second, the nature of information goods varies, making it difficult to price. For example, information can be raw data such as the number of cars passing by a road in a 24-hour cycle or an algorithm that analyzes traffic data and calculates the fastest route to drive. An algorithm may be easier to be commodified for commercial use but the raw data are still needed to feed data to the algorithm. Third, skills may matter more than labor time to produce information, so labor time may not determine exchange value of information. For example, a data entry job that requires little skills will not pay as much as a statistician job that analyzes the data. When information, as an intangible and inexhaustible goods, is so peculiar, how do information companies price their good? One strategy they use is to create an artificial scarcity. We will see how this works in the following sections.

MARKET STRUCTURE AND INTELLECTUAL PROPERTY

We can put a price on goods because they are scarce. There is not an unlimited amount of food and cars so they come with a price. In contrast, there are resources that are unlimited, such as air, sunlight, and water (Garnham, 1979; Ghosh, 2005a; Love & Hubbard, 2005; Schiller, 1988). As such, these resources are free to all living creatures. These are common goods that all lives can enjoy. In fact, it'd be immoral to deprive any living creatures of them. Among resources shared by humans, some unlimited ones are love and knowledge: parents can love all their children regardless of how many there are, teachers can lecture to as many students as possible. However, these intangible resources may be constrained by tangible resources, such as the number of toys for children or the size of the lecture hall.

Nevertheless, digital media may eliminate these limitations because they enable the reproduction and distribution of information in different spaces and times. For example, a copy of a video game can be played many times by multiple users; a lecture can be live streamed to as many students as possible. If digital media allow an unlimited resource—information, in this case—to be used by an unlimited number of users in different places and time, then should this resource be free, like sunlight, air, and love?

Political economists (Babe, 1995) believe that information should be treated as a public resource that is freely available to users. Because one person's consumption of information does not deprive others from using it, so it does not suffer from the problem of scarcity. Therefore information can be priced very low, if not free (Abramson, 2005). However, this is clearly not the case about digital information, in some cases digital information is very expensive. For example, computer software is expensive; specialized information such as financial information and medical information is out of reach for the average person; and education in some countries is expensive as well.

To explain why the cost of information is high despite digital technologies, we have to first understand the role that corporations play in developing digital technologies and information, two business models that impose scarcity of digital information, and finally how intellectual property laws protect private interests.

Information Technologies Development and Market Structure

It is well-documented that the Internet was developed by the U.S. military during the Cold War (Bermejo, 2007). After the technology was de-militarized, academics had the opportunities to develop it further. John Perry Barlow, one of the Internet pioneers, believe that the Internet should be free from the control of government and corporations (Goldsmith & Wu, 2006). However, it did not take too long for corporations to take control of the Internet and digital technologies; they did it upon the encouragement of government (Schiller, 1999). For example, the information highway initiative during the Clinton Administration encouraged corporations to develop digital technologies for commercial purpose.

Nowadays, information technology companies are some of the largest corporations in the world. For example, among the 50 U.S. corporations with the largest revenue, 11 of them are information and digital technology companies: Amazon.com, Apple, AT&T, Alphabet, Verizon Communications, Microsoft, Comcast, Dell Technologies, IBM, Intel, and Facebook ("Fortune 500", n/a). From time to time, there are newcomers that challenge the power of established companies, but these newcomers became major players as well. Google, Facebook, and Apple were once seen as challengers to establishments such as Microsoft and IBM, but they soon behave exactly like these companies, wielding more power in the market. U.S. politicians who belong to different camps agree that Google and Facebook have too much power, essentially monopolizing the markets (McChesney, Wood, & Foster, 1998) and making them less competitive.

However, in reality, these corporations may not compete with each other as much as politicians are willing to believe. They all depend on information technologies and they often patronize each other for technologies. For example, consumers may see Amazon.com as an online retailer who competes with other big retailers, such as Walmart and Target, but Amazon also provides web services for some of the largest corporations, such as Comcast, Disney, Dow Jones, Netflix, and Sony (Saunders, 2020).

Lastly, even though different information and computing technologies corporations may appear to compete with each other, each of them dominates a certain market. Therefore, the markets for digital information and computing technologies and digital information are at most characterized as an oligopoly but each of them has a dominating company (Abramson, 2005). For example, in the U.S., three companies captured almost 90 percent of the smartphone market (Apple, Samsung, and LG) ("U.S. smartphone market share", n/a). Globally, three search engines dominated 95 percent of the desktop search market (Alphabet's Google, Microsoft's bing, and Verizon's Yahoo) ("Worldwide desktop market share", n/a).

The market structure of computing technologies and digital information means these corporations can wield power to influence how the public sees information and to limit governments' involvement in democratizing information. Both of them directly relate to pricing. To access information, consumers either need pay for it or watch ads before accessing free information. Neither option allows for truly free information. The power of these corporations also means they see themselves as main drivers of the economy, they can have an upper hand in lobbying governments in market regulation.

Two Models of Commodified Information

Two popular models for corporations to commodify information are a subscription-based model and an advertising model (Schiller, 2007). Despite the different processes of information commodification, both models exploit some producers and consumers.

In the first model, access to digital information requires a subscription, such as paying a monthly fee to an online streaming service or newspaper. Paying for an online subscription is similar to paying for a subscription to cable television, the consumers partially pay for the content. The subscription fee will increase the media organization's revenue which in turn will be used to pay media producers. However, subscription fees are not sufficient to run media organizations. Most media organizations rely on advertising money to balance their accounts. In this subscription-based model, media consumers pay twice: first they pay the subscription fee, second they pay with their time and attention to read and watch the ads (Smythe, 1977). Unlike workers whose time is exchanged with money, media consumers also exchange their time with content even though they partially pay for the content.

Media producers are exploited in the commodification process as well. Digital media may allow their work to have a longer shelf life and a larger audience, but wider and longer exposure does not mean media producers make more money. For example, in 2007, film and television writers went on strike because media companies did not share with them profits from DVD sales. In the pre-digital era, sales of video cassette tapes accounted for marginal profits so writers did not complain about not getting a share. However, the explosion of the digital market meant consumers bought more DVDs for home consumption. The profits made from such sales, however, were not fairly shared with the writers. Media organizations argued that DVDs, like film trailers, are a form of promotion so the profits need not to be shared. Media corporations use a loophole in the pre-digital age to make a case to favor themselves even though consumers' habits have clearly changed.

A subscription model also applies to specialized content and software for businesses. In some markets, there are only a few major players so they can set the subscription fee high. For example, there are only four companies in the U.S. that lease computer terminals for finance professionals. Because of the lack of competition, annual subscription fee could cost as much as US$20,000 ("Bloomberg vs. Capital IQ", n/a). Unlike online streaming services where they set the cost low to attract a large number of subscribers, specialized information firms set the price high so as to maintain exclusivity. In this case, information scarcity is artificially created so that few could afford it. Another example is higher education institutions. A lot of students and their parents complain about the skyrocketing cost of higher education. Some asked why the cost of education is high when free online materials are easy to find. While most focus their attention on fancy residential halls and athletic facilities, few look at the high cost of software and database subscriptions. Tuition money also goes to subscriptions for general and specialized software, library databases, as well as a myriad of data management systems for administrative purposes. Some of these information management systems are oligopolies. For example, the four most popular learning management systems (Blackboard, Brightspace, Canvas, and Moodle) account for 90 percent of the market in the U.S. (McKenzie, 2018). The lack of competition means higher education institutions have few choices but to pay the price; the cost is then transferred to the students and their parents. Critics of higher education costs are correct on one count: that any person could learn with free online resources, but they have not pointed out the cost of proprietary software subscriptions needed to run a modern education institution.

The second model to commodify information is "free" information provided by users' activities. The Internet has offered an unprecedented opportunity for information sharing: not only can content producers upload content for others to consume without paying a subscription, but there can also be more diverse content. The earliest Internet has indeed created a "wild wild web" with user-generated content, no gatekeeping, little government oversight, and little commercial interest. However, since the Internet became commercialized, it was soon dominated by private corporations with website owners selling ad space, search engine companies mixing paid ads with organic search results, social media companies selling users' data, and news websites selling space to sponsors' content.

In the cases of social media and search engine corporations, they do not produce original content, they only provide platforms for users to generate content. In a sense, they provide a "free" service to users who in exchange agree to be shown ads and have their data sold (Fuchs, 2011a). The handsome revenues generated from selling the audience to advertisers (Smythe, 1977), marketers and data firms are not shared with the users (Gandy, 1995). While some may argue that looking at ads is beneficial to users because they gain knowledge of new products, political economists have argued that looking at ads is an exploitative practice. Their argument is as follows: users need to spend time and attention to look at ads, therefore looking at ads is a form of labor (Jhally & Livant, 1986). These users spend some part of the day selling their labor time in exchange for wage. When they are off work, their time is commodified by search engine and social media companies who "buy" their time in exchange of free services (Jhally & Livant, 1986; Wasser, 2001). Unlike the workers who can stop selling labor time to one employer by quitting the jobs, they have fewer choices when it comes to online information consumption (see Harvey, 1982): they can refuse to use services that come with ads or they can subscribe to some services that are ad-free, such as an online streaming service. This brings us back to the first business model: subscription-based. Some may disagree that the consumers are exploited, they may argue that consumers now have more options, including pirated content. This brings into question why intellectual property of information should be seen as private property (Baker, McKenzie, & Hart, 1998; Coombe, 1994).

Intellectual Property Protection

Most information companies do not sell tangible products, they sell intangible products. Therefore, the most valuable assets are not their products, but intellectual property of their content and algorithm. Information produced by corporations is all copyrighted, violation of copyrights could lead to a fine or even jail time. Inventions by themselves as executives. As executives, their compensation is tied to how well the company's stocks perform in the financial market. In this case, the value that these executives create matter much less than the hours that they put in, but how much value the companies are speculated to make in the future. In this sense, their compensation has little to do with the value that they have produced but the value that is speculated. It is similar to gamblers buying themselves expensive gifts because they speculate how much they will win. However, unlike gamblers who put their financial health at risk, speculation of companies' future performance has profound implications on working conditions throughout the supply chain. For example, even though President Trump has asked Apple to move manufacturing back to the U.S., the high labor cost will lead to expensive products. Any companies that move manufacturing back to the States will probably suffer from a sharp drop in market value because speculators expect these companies will not be as competitive as their counterparts that use cheaper labor. Therefore, labor exploitation is necessary to safeguard information executives' handsome compensation. The value of information, as defined in capitalism, has profound impacts on who earns what regardless of the amount of labor time.

ALTERNATIVES TO PRIVATIZED INFORMATION

I began this chapter by differentiating use value from exchange value. I then argued that unlike tangible and exhaustible goods, information is intangible and inexhaustible, hence it is impossible to assign an exchange value to information. Therefore, information should be treated as public resources; it is more similar to air and sunlight than cars and houses. Yet, information is one of the more expensive goods in the market. Two reasons why it has a high exchange value is because of the oligopolistic market structure and privatized intellectual property.

To counter privatized information controlled by corporations, some artists and activists argue that privatized information controlled by corporations does not benefit the public because it stifles creativity (Ghosh, 2005a). Because of all the legal restrictions, humans are not able to stand on the shoulders of giants and build upon human knowledge based on previous work. To challenge privatized information, I examine two areas of work that artists and activists have been doing to increase the commons.

Artists challenge privatized information by testing the boundary of what kind and how much information can be appropriated for their creation. For example, DJs and hip-hop artists create music by mixing previous work, visual artists poke fun at commercial culture by taking advantage of the fair use doctrine which "promotes freedom of expression by permitting the unlicensed use of copyright-protected works" ("More information on fair use", n/a) when information is reproduced as criticism, comment, news reporting, teaching, scholarship, and research. However, this doctrine does not mean that artists and activists are protected from being suited by copyrights owners. Below I summarize three lawsuits to illustrate the circumstances under which fair use is upheld by the court.

In one case, a book publisher crowdfunded a publication in which two culturally significant texts, *Star Trek* and Dr. Seuss's books, had a mashup. Dr. Seuss Enterprises sued the author for illegally using copyrighted materials. Upon examining the comic book, the court decided that the author had borrowed elements from both original texts but had significantly transformed them. The court also believed that the adaptation targeted a slightly adult market so potential consumers will not be mistaken that the new creative work is the same as the original one (Gardner, 2019).

In another case, a photographer sued the Andy Warhol Foundation for using a picture that she took of the artist Prince by appropriating it in a piece of artwork. The court was in favor of the Warhol Foundation because the new work advanced visual art and thus added value to the public interest. The court also ruled that the artist had transformed the photographed subject, Prince, from a "vulnerable human being" to someone "iconic, larger than life figure". Lastly, the court believed that the piece of art is immediately recognized as Warhol's piece rather than the original photograph ("Andy Warhol found", n/a).

In the third case, a spoken word recording by rapper Jimmy Smith was sampled in a song by hip-hop artist Drake. The court ruled in favor of Drake because he did not directly use the quote but delete and rearrange some words, thus changing the meaning of Smith's quote. The court further suggested that Drake added something new to the message and thus transformed it (Minsker, 2017).

In all the above cases, the court was not primarily concerned with the commercial nature of the original or the derived work, It also was not concerned with the intentions of the artists. The court mostly concerned whether the new work has transformed the original work, giving it new meanings and adding value to public interest. If all the cases had not been protected by the fair use doctrine, art could not thrive because artists could not make comments on previous work or pay homage to other artists.

Some activists chose to challenge privatized information in another path, seeking new ways to share the commons: the Free/Open Source movement challenges proprietary software by arguing that computer code can only be effective if the crowd contributes to the commons. The Copyleft movement challenges privatized intellectual property by setting up alternative models for creators to share their work. Both movements believe that use value should take priority over exchange value of information; creators and users should be empowered with contributing to the commons; abundance rather than scarcity of information should be emphasized; and the commons can only thrive in the absence of competition (Raymond, 2001; van Wendel de Joode, de Brceiju, & van Eeten, 2003; Weber, 2004).

Richard Stallman (2000), one of the earliest advocates of free source, argued that in order to improve computer code, the code should be made public so that the crowd can contribute to its constant improvement. Most of the code published by corporations is proprietary because these corporations own the intellectual property. Users cannot view or modify the code. Protected code becomes a problem when the bugs in the software cause it to crash. Very often end users will send a report to the developers who will then fix the bugs and release new code. However, the improvement depends on the skills of a limited number of developers who may or may not release the new code. To Richard Stallman, improvement of code relies on freedom that allows all skilled developers to modify flawed code.

Even though most end users may not have heard of open source, they interact with it when they go online. Linux, an open source code, is an alternative to two proprietary operating systems: Microsoft Windows and macOS. Linux is the operating system used by organizations such as the National Aeronautics and Space Administration (NASA) and the U.S. Department of Defense. In addition, a wide range of consumer gadgets also run on Linux, such as the handheld device Amazon's Kindle and self-driving cars. Lastly, online sites such as Instagram and Netflix also run on Linux (Sneddon, 2019).

In addition to the movement of open source code, there is also a movement to provide an alternative system of intellectual property. For example, Creative Commons licenses allow creators to choose how their intellectual property can be protected. Creative Commons founder, Lawrence Lessig, a vocal critic of privatized intellectual property (Lessig, 2014), believes that current laws stifles creativity, which is detrimental to a thriving commons. Creative Commons then aims to build "a globally-accessible public commons of knowledge and culture" by allowing creators to share their work while using others' work. The sharing of commons is believed to build "a more equitable, accessible, and innovative world" ("What we do", n/a). Individual creators and institutions can choose one of the six licences, each of them allows users to do a variety of things. The license that has the least restriction is "the creative commons public domain dedication"; with this license, creators choose to give up their copyright and offer their work for the public domain globally. This license allows users to distribute, remix, adapt, and build upon the public domain materials in any medium or format. The most restricted kind allows users to copy and distribute the material in any medium or format but does not allow for alteration. The users also cannot use the work for commercial purposes and should credit the creators for the work ("About CC licenses", n/a).

Why would code developers and content creators share their work without compensation? Why would some give their creation out for free? These questions are central to re-thinking what information is. As I have argued throughout this chapter, information is an inexhaustible resource, similar to sunlight and air. Yet, we are paying an exorbitant amount of money for information because this exchange value is set by a few powerful corporations. This exchange value is *arbitrary* because it is neither measured by labor time spent on producing the goods nor calculated based on prices of raw materials. Nevertheless, we have been trained by the logic of capitalism; we have come to accept the market logic that producers need to charge for their goods and consumers need to pay for them. We do not usually ask what if the market logic is not the best way to allocate resources.

There are many situations in life where this market logic does not apply (John, 2017). For example, we volunteer our time and donate money for social causes in which we believe; we help our neighbors when they are in need; we share food with our friends and family members; we form hobby groups to support each other. Code developers and content producers who want to contribute to the commons operate in the same way: some share their creation because they believe information should belong to the commons (Benkler, 2005, 2006); some share their talents because they believe others need their help; some see sharing as an opportunity for collaboration and improvement; some want to increase their social capital in their peer groups (Ghosh, 2005b; Lakhani & Wolf, 2005). These motivations all show that creators believe their work is useful for others, therefore use value takes primacy over exchange value. The ability to create is innately human; to create is to be human.

CONCLUSION

Digital technologies have caused an explosion of information because they enable those who have digital literacies to produce and consume online content. While technologies offer the possibility to create an online repertoire of human knowledge, the possibility has been limited when information is controlled by a few powerful corporations that follow the market logic. This logic asks content producers—professionals and amateurs—to see their creation as commodities. This logic also excludes a large number of populations from accessing information. From a political economic of communication perspective, I explain why information, being an intangible and inexhaustible goods, has become an expensive commodity. This perspective highlights the historical development of the new information and communication technologies in developed countries: even though new information and communication technologies were developed with public money, corporations have quickly developed a market and gained control of the development. The few corporations that share the information market can decide how much to charge for information. They are able to set a high price to information because of the oligopolistic market structure that has eliminated real competition. Intellectual property laws that favor privatized information also protects corporations, not consumers. Both market structure and intellectual property not only probe the public to see themselves as consumers, but they also exploit workers in the global supply chain. Artists and activists have challenged the market logic by pointing out how arbitrary intellectual property laws can be. Lawsuits about fair use sometimes show the court is sympathetic with creators who build their work by appropriating previously published content. Open source and Copyleft movements show that activists offer new ways to rebuild the commons by building up networks and mechanisms for the public to share their resources and talents.

BIBLIOGRAPHY

About CC licenses. Creative Commons. Retrieved from: https://creativecommons.org/about/cclicenses/

Abramson, B. (2005). *Digital phoenix: Why the information economy collapsed and how it will rise again*. Cambridge, MA: MIT Press.

Alikhan, S., & Mashelkar, R. (2004). *Intellectual property and competitive strategies in the 21st century*. The Hague, the Netherlands: Kluwer Law International.

Alphabet. (2019). *Annual report to the United States Securities and Exchange Commission*. Mountain View, CA: Alphabet.

Andy Warhol Found. for the Visual Arts, Inc. v. Goldsmith17-cv-2532 (JGK), 2019 U.S. Dist. LEXIS 110086 (S.D.N.Y. July 1, 2019). Retrieved from: https://www.copyright.gov/fair-use/summaries/andywarhol-goldsmith-sdny2019.pdf

Babe, R. E. (1995). *Communication and the transformation of economics: Essays in information, public policy, and political economy*. Boulder, CO: Westview Press.

Babe, R. E. (1996). Economics and information: Toward a new (and more sustainable) worldview. *Canadian Journal of Communication*, 21(2), 161–178.

Baek, J. (2016). *North Korea's hidden revolution: How the information underground is transforming a closed society*. New Haven, CT: Yale University Press.

Baker & McKenzie, & Hart, R. J. (1998). *Guide to intellectual property in the I.T. industry* (1st ed.). London: Sweet and Maxwell.

Bates, B. J. (1988). Information as an economic good: Sources of individual and social value. In V. Mosco & J. Wasko (Eds.), *The political economy of information* (pp. 76–94). Madison, WI: University of Wisconsin Press.

Benkler, Y. (2005). Coase's penguin, or, Linux and the nature of the firm. In J. Feller, B. Fitzgerald, S. A. Hissam, & K. R. Lakhani (Eds.), *Perspectives on free and open source software* (pp. 169–206). Cambridge, MA: MIT Press.

Benkler, Y. (2006). *The wealth of networks: How social production transforms markets and freedom*. New Haven, CT: Yale University Press.

Bermejo, F. (2007). *The Internet audience: Constitution and measurement*. New York: Peter Lang.

Bhuiyan, J. (2018, February 9). Uber and Alphabet have settled their self-driving lawsuit with a $245 million equity payout. *Vox*. Retrieved from: https://www.vox.com/2018/2/9/16993598/uber-waymo-alphabet-self-driving-settle-lawsuit-245-million-payout

Bloomberg vs. Capital IQ vs. FactSet vs. Thomson Reuters Eikon. *Wall Street Prep*. Retrieved from: https://www.wallstreetprep.com/knowledge/bloomberg-vs-capital-iq-vs-factset-vs-thomson-reuters-eikon/

Coombe, R. J. (1994). Objects of property and subjects of politics: Intellectual property laws and democratic dialogue. In D. Patterson (Ed.), *Postmodernism and laws* (pp. 275–302). New York: New York University Press.

Drahos, P. (2002). Introduction. In P. Drahos & R. Mayne (Eds.). *Global intellectual property rights: Knowledge, access and development* (pp. 1–9). Hampshire, UK: Palgrave and Oxfam UK.

Eisenstein, Z. (1998). *Global obscenities: Patriarchy, capitalism and the lure of cyberfantasy*. New York: New York University Press.

Fascinating facts. Library of Congress. Retrieved from: https://www.loc.gov/about/fascinating-facts/

Fortune 500. *Fortune*. Retrieved from: https://fortune.com/fortune500/2020/search/

Fuchs, C. (2011a). A contribution to the critique of the political economy of Google. *Fast Capitalism, 8*(1). Retrieved from: https://www.uta.edu/huma/agger/fastcapitalism/8_1/fuchs8_1.html

Fuchs, C. (2011b). *Foundations of critical media and information studies*. London: Routledge.

Fuchs, C. (2013). Theorising and analysing digital labor: From global value chains to modes of production. *The Political Economy of Communication, 2*(1), 3–27.

Fuchs, C., & Mosco, V. (2012). Introduction: Marx is back—The importance of Marxist theory and research for critical communication studies today. *Triple C: Cognition, Communication, Co-operation, 10*(2), 127–140.

Gandy. O. H. (1993). Toward a political economy of personal information. *Critical Studies in Mass Communication, 10*(1), 70–97.

Gandy, O. H. (1995). Tracking the audience: Personal information and privacy. In J. Downing, A. Mohammadi, & A. Sreberry-Mohammadi (Eds.), *Questioning the media: A critical introduction* (pp. 221–237). Thousand Oaks, CA: Sage.

Gardner, E. (2019, March 12). "Star Trek"/Dr. Seuss mashup deemed copyright fair use by judge. *The Hollywood Reporter*. Retrieved from: https://www.hollywoodreporter.com/thr-esq/star-trek-dr-seuss-mashup-deemed-a-fair-use-by-judge-1194166

Garnham, N. (1979). Contribution to a political economy of mass-communication. *Media, Culture and Society, 1*(1), 123–146.

General information. Library of Congress. Retrieved from: https://www.loc.gov/about/general-information/

Ghosh, R. A. (2005a). Why collaboration is important (again). In R. A. Ghosh (Ed.), *Code: Collaborative ownership and the digital economy* (pp. 1–11). Cambridge, MA: MIT Press.

Ghosh, R. A. (2005b). Understanding free software developers: Findings from the FLOSS study. In J. Feller, B. Fitzgerald, S. A. Hissam, & K. R. Lakhani (Eds.),

Perspectives on free and open source software (pp. 23–45). Cambridge, MA: MIT Press.
Goldsmith, J., & Wu, T. (2006). *Who controls the Internet? Illusions of a borderless world*. Oxford: Oxford University Press.
Harvey, D. (1982). *The limits to capital*. Chicago: University of Chicago Press.
Harvey, D. (2010). *A companion to Marx's capital*. New York: Verso.
Heydebrand, W. (2003). The time dimension in Marxian social theory. *Time and Society*, 12(2/3), 147–188.
Industries and sectors. International Labour Organization. Retrieved from: https://www.ilo.org/global/industries-and-sectors/lang-en/index.htm
Jhally, S., & Livant, B. (1986). Watching as working: The valorization of audience consciousness. *Journal of Communication, 36*(3), 124–143.
John, N. A. (2017). *The age of sharing*. Cambridge, MA: Polity.
Karaganis, J. (2011). (Ed.). *Media piracy in emerging economies*. New York: Social Science Research Council.
Klinger, B. (2010). Contraband cinema: Piracy, "Titanic", and Central Asia. *Cinema Journal, 49*(2), 106–124.
Lakhani, K. R., & Wolf, R. G. (2005). Why hackers do what they do: Understanding motivation and efforts in free/open source software projects. In J. Heller, B. Fitzgerald, S. A. Hissan, & K. R. Lakhani (Eds.), *Perspectives on free and open source software* (pp. 3–21). Cambridge, MA: MIT Press.
Lessig, L. (2001). *The future of ideas: The fate of the commons in a connected world*. New York: Random House.
Lessig, L. (2014) *Free culture: How big media uses technology and the law to lock down culture and control creativity*. New York: Penguin.
Love, J., & Hubbard, T. (2005). Paying for public goods. In J. Feller, B. Fitzgerald, S. A. Hissam, & K. R. Lakhani (Eds.), *Perspectives on free and open source software* (pp. 207–229). Cambridge, MA: MIT Press.
Marx, K. (1999). *Capital: A critique of political economy*. Marxists.org. Retrieved from: https://www.marxists.org/archive/marx/works/1867-c1/
May, C. (2002). *The information society: A sceptical view*. Cambridge, UK: Polity.
McChesney, R. W., Wood, E. M., & Foster, J. B. (Eds.) (1988). *Capitalism and the information age: The political economy of the global communication revolution*. New York: The Monthly Press.
McKenzie, L. (2018, July 10). Canvas catches, and may be passes, Blackboard. *Inside Higher Ed*. Retrieved from: https://www.insidehighered.com/digital-learning/article/2018/07/10/canvas-catches-and-maybe-passes-blackboard-top-learning
Minsker, E. (2017, June 1). Drake beats lawsuit over "pound cake/Paris Morton Music 2" sample. *Pitchfork*. Retrieved from: https://pitchfork.com/news/73897-drake-beats-lawsuit-over-pound-cakeparis-morton-music-2-sample/
More information on fair use. Copyright.gov. Retrieved from: https://www.copyright.gov/fair-use/more-info.html
Number of Alphabet (Google) patent families worldwide by filing year from 1998 to 2018, by legal status. *Statista*. Retrieved from: https://www.statista.com/statistics/

1033921/number-of-alphabet-google-patents-by-filing-year-and-status-worldwide/
Occupational employment statistics. U.S. Bureau of Labor Statistics. Retrieved from: https://www.bls.gov/oes/tables.htm
Perzanowski, A., & Schultz, J. (2016). *The end of ownership: Personal property in the digital economy.* Cambridge, MA: MIT Press.
Postone, M. (1993). *Time, labor, and social domination: A reinterpretation of Marx's critical theory.* Cambridge, UK: Cambridge University Press.
Preda, A. (2009). *Information, knowledge and economic life: An introduction to the sociology of markets.* Oxford, UK: Oxford University Press.
Raymond, E. S. (2001). *The cathedral and the bazaar: Musings on Linux and open source by an accidental revolutionary* (rev. ed.). Sebastopol, CA: O'Reilly.
Roberts, K., & Webster, F. (1988). Cybernetic capitalism: Information, technology, everyday life. In V. Mosco & J. Wasko (Eds.), *The political economy of information* (pp. 44–75). Madison, WI: University of Wisconsin Press.
Saunders, B. (2020, January 28). Who's using Amazon Web Services? [2020 update]. *Contino.* Retrieved from: https://www.contino.io/insights/whos-using-aws
Schiller, D. (1988). How to think about information? In V. Mosco & J. Wasko (Eds.), *The political economy of information* (pp. 27–41). Madison, WI: University of Wisconsin Press.
Schiller, D. (1999). *Digital capitalism: Networking the global market system.* Cambridge, MA: MIT Press.
Schiller, D. (2007). *How to think about information.* Urbana, IL: University of Illinois Press.
Smythe, D. W. (1977). Communications: Blindspot of Western Marxism. *Canadian Journal of Political and Social Theory, 1*(3), 1–27.
Sneddon, J. (2019, July 30). Must read: 25 awesome things powered by Linux. *OMG! Ubuntu!* Retrieved from: https://www.omgubuntu.co.uk/2016/08/25-awesome-unexpected-things-powered-linux
Stallman, R. (2000). *GNU Emacs manual.* San Jose, CA: iUniverse.com.
Trump to combat movie piracy by China, saving the US economy $600B annually. (2018, March 15). *Fox Business.* Retrieved from: https://www.foxbusiness.com.
US smartphone market share: By quarter. Counterpoint. Retrieved from: https://www.counterpointresearch.com/us-market-smartphone-share/
Vaidhyanathan, S. (2007). The Googlization of everything and the future of copyright. *University of California, Davis Law Review, 40,* 1207–1231.
van Wendel de Joode, R., de Brceiju, J. A., & van Eeten, M. J. G. (2003). *Protecting the virtual commons: Self-organizing open source and free software communities and innovative intellectual property regimes.* The Hague, the Netherlands: T. M. C. Asser Press.
Wasser, F. (2001). Media is driving work. *M/C: A Journal of Media and Culture, 4*(5). Retrieved from: http://www.media-culture.org.au/0111/wasser.xml
Weber, S. (2004). *The success of open source.* Cambridge, MA: Harvard University Press.

What we do. Creative Commons. Retrieved from: https://creativecommons.org/about/

World Intellectual Property Organization (WIPO). *What is intellectual property*. Geneva, Switzerland: WIPO.

Worldwide desktop market share of leading search engines from January 2010 to January 2020. *Statista*. Retrieved from: https://www.statista.com/statistics/216573/worldwide-market-share-of-search-engines/

7

CONCLUSION
CAN WE DO MORE WITH INFORMATION?

INTRODUCTION

This book began by asking readers to observe how commuters interact with information during a subway ride. Even though the ride is short, commuters interact with different types of information. Some may find the types, amount, and speed of information so overwhelming that they, ironically, use technology to cope with the explosion of information. This book does not see information as something with which we cope, it instead sees *information as a possibility*. For this reason, this book wants its readers to dream of a better way to interact with information.

To dream of a better way, we need to first assess how we interact with information. From Chapters 2 to 6, I guided readers to focus on different ways to interact with information: we began with defining, then searching, accessing, using, and ended at creating. The questions that I asked throughout the chapters are: *who* has the *power* to design and control how we interact with information, *how* these decisions impact our political, economic, cultural and social lives, and *how* gender, race, and class differentiates experiences with information.

These questions are important to ask because asking them enables us to imagine what *more* we can do with information instead of what to do with *more* information.

If we only think about what to do with *more* information, we remain passive in coping with an ever-growing amount and speed of information. We will continue feeling overwhelmed with the choices in the marketplace. This passive position limits us to ask a narrow set of questions, such as what the best products in the market are, how to best cope with information, and how to protect online privacy.

In contrast, we take an active position when we ask what *more* we can do with information. A critical perspective will empower readers to make transformative changes when we understand how power works through the production, distribution, and consumption of information. In addition, we will understand how our agency will make us artists, critics, and activists who dare to imagine how information can be better.

In this concluding chapter, I ask readers to take up an active position and challenge them to take up a simple charge, which is to imagine ourselves as a commuter who occupies a very different social location from the one that we currently have. According to Anthias (2012), the term "social location" avoids the pitfall of the "social group" concept: "Our 'location' is embedded in relations of hierarchy within a multiplicity of specific situational and conjunctural spheres"; furthermore "locations relate to stratification (at local, national and transnational fields", within a contextual and chronologic context [by inhabiting] a 'real time and place' context" (p. 130). This charge has three parts: first, we imagine ourselves to be another person who interacts with information differently; second, we assess how various social locations differentiate experience with information; third, we take an active role in designing and controlling how we interact with information. But the privilege of taking up another social position comes with two ground rules: first, we are not superior to the person whose social location we will soon occupy. Second, we do not judge how this person uses information and why this person uses information in such a way. By observing these two ground rules, we will understand how gender, race, class, geographical locations, and other factors constitute this person's interactions with information.

When we take up an active position, we can imagine how our interaction with information can lead to better and more meaningful purposes. We can then afford to ask a wider set of questions. For example, why does one commuter rely on a smartphone to access online learning materials? What constraints does this person have when using a cell phone to do homework? Why is online learning promoted to be a career advancement shortcut even though most students drop out? In another example, if we occupy the position of a commuter whose first language is not English, what kinds of apps and sites will she likely use? Will she feel disconnected in an online environment that is predominantly English? Will she be able to create information that is meaningful to those who speak the same language (Munyua, 2000; Radloff & Primo, 2002)?

To imagine a different social location requires us to ask three questions: (1) Is more and faster information always better?; (2) What do we mean by better and more meaningful way to use information?; (3) How can readers see themselves as creators, critics, and activists of information? Before answering them, we first review four enduring issues stated in the introduction. The first enduring issue is information divides. This concept used to be narrowly defined as the gap between those who have access to technologies and those who have not, but it has been widened to include not only access to devices, but also technological competency. In addition, more attention has been paid to the structures that divide the "have" and "have not" populations. Information divides are not individual problems such as an unwillingness to learn technologies, but structural problems such as poverty and illiteracy. By broadening the definition, information divides reflect and constitute socioeconomic inequities.

The second enduring issue is who has the power to define, create, and commodify information. In all the chapters, we learn that institutions such as corporations and governments have more power to design and control information. We also learn that humans are not the only agencies, technologies also have a sense of agency that probes humans to do certain things. They are neither passive objects waiting to be used nor simply conduits of information. It is also important to acknowledge that power can be positive because it can bring significant transformations.

The third enduring issue is that information is not neutral and objective, it is politically, economically, socially, and culturally biased. The questions are then: Who has the authority to make biased information appear to be neutral? What are the implications of applying biased information to make decisions that affect the majority of the population?

The fourth enduring issue is social change and resistance. Even though individuals may appear to have less power than institutions such as governments and corporations, individuals have the agency to effect social change and exercise resistance. If we look back in human history, social groups struggled to unsettle power relations between those who had power and those who had less. Mass education and the public library are two examples of how large-scaled changes can bring widespread literacy to most of the populations. On a smaller scale, social movements such as open source and copyleft have provided real alternatives to market-based intellectual property laws. Even though this book has pointed out the power that institutions have over information, it is very likely that collective actions would bring positive changes. But first, there needs to be a discussion about what the positive changes are.

QUESTION 1: IS MORE AND FASTER INFORMATION ALWAYS BETTER?

Most information services and technology companies advertise their products as having fast speed, large storage space, and powerful functions. These selling points imply that more and faster information is preferred to less and slower information. The question is why more and faster information is better. To answer this question, let's look at how Apple Computers markets the latest MacBook Air model. This latest model is said to be "thin" and "light" but "more powerful" because of "faster graphics" and twice the storage capacity. Apple explained that these features are desirable because images on the screen are more detailed and texts are sharper; users can multi-task from web browsing, game-playing and video-editing. users can store more movies, music, photos, files, and games. Matched with a low price point, these attractive features lure consumers to upgrade their computer even though their old models work just fine.

As a user of a seven-year-old MacBook Air, these features do sound appealing to me. However, it is also obvious that a faster laptop with larger storage capacity does not automatically make me a better writer and teacher. Similarly, most students do not need a fast laptop to be effective learners. In fact, if purchasing a new laptop would make one a productive worker and an efficient learner, then there is no need to spend any effort on working and learning. If there is no strong correlation between more and faster information with better writing, teaching, and learning, then why are consumers so ready to accept the myth that more and faster information is desirable?

The myth that more and faster information is better needs to be understood in the logic of capitalism. Growth is a capitalist mantra. A successful company is one that experiences steady growth in sales, revenue, profit, and the number of employees. Similarly, a good economy is one that steadily grows in size. Growth is measured in strictly quantifiable term. If some qualities—such as diversity and inclusion among employees—cannot be measured, then these qualities are not seen to add value to a company.

If some qualities cannot be quantified, then the capitalistic solution is to quantify them so that they can be measured. Once qualities are quantified, the success of one company can be compared to others. Magazines such as *Fortune* and *Forbes* have created numerous lists to rank the best companies in the U.S. and the world. Companies that are ranked high on lists became models that appear to run their business on a working formula. For companies that are not ranked so high on the list, they can look at the success formula and try to replicate others' success. These rankings are empirical observation, yet they become formulae to predict which companies will succeed or not.

The above is not the only piece of evidence where the capitalist logic of growth redresses an empirical observation as a law of nature. In the middle of 1960s, Gordon Moore noticed that the number of transistors in an integrated circuit doubled every two years. He neither predicted that this growth will persist nor suggested that it is a law. Yet, Moore's law has been appropriated out of context and it is regarded as a rule that computing capacity doubles every two years. Because this observation became a law of nature, companies in the information and technologies industries race to fulfill this prophecy. Consumers have also come to believe that this prophecy will be fulfilled. Therefore, computing devices that are only a few years old are deemed to be too slow and outdated for ever faster and more information. By this logic, my seven-year-old laptop is seen to be too slow for any good work.

The implications of this belief have a profound impact on an understanding of information in all societies. I will discuss two here: first, quantified information is believed to be automatically neutral; second, the progress of any information society is linear (Postone, 1993). Quantified information is assumed to be neutral. Because it is neutral, it is assumed to be objective. For example, weather reports are supposed to present an unbiased account of forecasts; when weather forecasters say it will be hot today, it is not a subjective opinion but an objective fact that can be independently observed and verified. However, I have argued that even though different thermometers may show approximately the same temperature, the use of Fahrenheit in the U.S. shows its self-perceived exceptionalism. Moreover, in Chapter 5, "Using", I have shown that quantified data, such as those in U.S. census, may not be so objective. Racial and ethnic designations show that the white race is the norm; non-white populations have to choose their designations based on white people's views of themselves. In addition, census-takers could once decide others' race and ethnicity based on physical appearance. Even though the U.S. census now allows for self-identification, how one identifies with a race or ethnicity is not objective. For example, a mixed-race person of white and black origins would see themselves as Blacks but mixed-race Cubans would see themselves as whites. In another example, artificial intelligence may be racially biased: facial recognition technologies immediately classify dark-skinned women as not creditworthy (Totty, 2020).

I have also pointed out in Chapter 5, "Using", that private corporations such as social media and computing companies have more resources to quantify information and to apply them in a speedy way. Big Data technology converts digital information of different types into homogeneous data. These data can then be directly fed into an algorithm which can automatically make decisions about course of actions. In the absence of human interpretation, Big Data can have negative implications on society. For example, in the 2016 U.S. Presidential Election, Russian Government-directed trolls could directly place ads to dissuade black voters from participating in the election. Even though Facebook later changed its policies of foreign government-sponsored online trolls, the company still relies on Big Data technology to foster revenue growth by selling more ads in a shorter time frame. Human interpretation of data is deemed too slow

CONCLUSION 177

and inaccurate to make decisions even though some decisions have profound implications on society, such as electing a president.

In Chapter 5, "Using", I also showed that quantified information is not neutral because those who design the technology decide what kind of data to collect and what to ignore. When governments collect Big Data for surveillance, they can effectively control the movement of their citizens. For example, smart identity cards have the potential to violate civil liberty because state employees can view all citizens' data at once. In the case of the Chinese Government, the state can quickly track movements of its citizens through facial-recognition technology. The state can then quickly identify citizens who violate civil conducts. The dual technology facial recognition and tracking may suppress political activists whose movements are monitored by the state.

Quantified information is then hardly neutral because someone in power need to decide what information to collect, who to collect it, with what technologies it is collected, and how information leads them to make certain decisions. Rather than assuming that biased information can be made neutral, it is more appropriate to ask who has the power to *make information appear neutral* and what benefits they gain by pretending that information is neutral.

The second implication of the myth that faster and more information is better is that technological progress is assumed to be linear: that humans who live in society with slow and little information will move towards society of plenty information. This assumption of linear progress is also rooted in the capitalist logic because, as stated, constant growth is necessary to keep this political economic system running.

The concept of digital divide well illustrates the belief of linear progress. I mentioned in the introduction that there are gaps in the ownership of technological devices and competency in technological knowledge between different geographical regions, genders, races, ages, and social classes. International organizations, governments, corporations, and civil society are eager to bridge the gaps. But bridging the gaps does not mean those who have more need to give to those who have less; it also does not mean that those who have more need to reflect on why they have more. Bridging the gaps mainly fault those who have less for not catching up. Their job is then to catch up so that they are not left behind. Few questions are asked why technological devices and competency are unevenly distributed in the first place. In Chapter 4, "Accessing", I showed how international organizations strive to narrow the digital gaps between developed and developing economies because a country with more knowledge workers can lift the nation up from poverty. At a country level, the government bears the responsibility to increase its knowledge economy, sometimes promoting to women that knowledge jobs will lead to better-paying jobs.

If technological progress is not linear and an information society is not necessarily more advanced than other societies, then it opens up more questions. For example, are there more ways for a society to progress and for technology to advance? What if different kinds of information society co-exist? Can an information society run on a different political economic system (Cooks & Isgro, 2005)? When an information society is solely defined as one that has more and faster information, then we miss the opportunity to reimagine other kinds of society where information is less but more equitable among all members (Henwood, Wyatt, Miller, & Senker, 2000). Similar to an earlier point that we should ask who has the power to make data appear neutral, we should also ask who has the power to define what an information society is and how technologies are believed to move societies along a linear progression.

To conclude this section, I am not advocating that less and slower information is better than more and faster. I am advocating that we need to understand who has the power to define an information society, what role information plays in a society, and how technologies should develop in such a society. To counter a hegemonic way to think about information, we should see information as something heterogeneous and varying (Babe, 2011), we should accept that information is not only digital information that can be purified into quantitative data ready to be fed to an algorithm. If information is seen as heterogeneous and varying, then it is never neutral because information is always embedded with personal imprints, created in a specific space within a specific timeframe with different technologies that give it a specific quality and property (Harvey, 1989). By embracing the heterogeneity of information, we also accept that information can be produced in any political economic system, and the current dominant capitalist model is all but one.

QUESTION 2: WHAT DO WE MEAN BY "BETTER" INFORMATION?

In the previous section, I stated that there are many ways to think about an information society, some of them are not solely defined by more and faster information. In this section, I ask what other ways we can imagine the future of an information society. What may be "better" information? Will our visions of better information be similar or different? If yes, how can a community create and use information that will be better for everyone of us? (Hassan, 2008; Webster, 2006).

To imagine how better information will help us imagine an information society that is not solely defined by volume and speed of information, we need to first ask whether information is a means or an ends. If information is only a means to an ends, then what will be this ends? As an individual, I want information to help me make better decisions as a community member, as a member of the public, and as a consumer. I do not want information just for the sake of having information. For example, as a community member, I want to have information to know how I can better my fellow members; as a member of the public, I would like to know public opinion about different social issues; as a consumer, I want to know which products meet my needs.

Despite the volume and speed of online information, very often it is not good enough for me because most of the information *was produced within unbalanced social relations*. In addition, *this information exists to reinforce this power relation*. For example, there is a dwindling number of local newspapers. To learn about my community, I may need to rely on official information from the city hall or online sites that advertise local businesses. Unless I talk to community members, there are few ways to understand their concerns. Similarly, while Amazon seems to be an informative site to compare products, I understand that the products that occupy prominent places are there because the companies pay a fee to be prominently featured. Because of unbalanced relationships between commercial enterprises and community members, between advertisers and consumers, the "not good enough" information will not probe positive changes to community members, the public, and consumers. In the words of Crawford (1996), "mere information does not imply knowledge, nor does the latter necessarily entail power. To transform raw information into useful knowledge requires the application of values and the production of meaning" (p. 75).

If good information is narrowly defined as more and better information, then the breakneck speed in which information is produced, disseminated, and consumed would mask unequal social relations because the heady speed in which information travels asks us to accept false choices: if users are not satisfied with information provided by one party, then they can choose other provided by another party. As I mentioned in the Introduction, large corporations, in comparison to individuals, have unparalleled opportunity to influence how information is being produced, distributed, and consumed. I further showed in Chapter 5, "Using", that members of public may opt out of providing information, but they cannot decide how governments collect and use information.

We can only have better information when the producers, distributors, and consumers are aware that unbalanced power relations are embedded in the process. These social actors also recognize the non-neutral and heterogeneous nature of information. In addition, these actors understand that information is constitutive of both technology and society. To explain, all social relations are governed by power. Even if some social relations are claimed to be egalitarian, we reproduce them based on an historical understanding of that relationship. The key is to acknowledge such unbalanced power relations and to use power towards a positive end. For example, teachers have power over students because they design the class, regulate classroom behaviors, and assess students' learning. An egalitarian relationship between teachers and students does not usually work in a classroom. Instead of pretending that students have an equal power with teachers, teachers should ask themselves questions such as:

- whether they choose information with a wide range of viewpoints;
- whether they deliberately withhold information because they do not feel comfortable with it or do not want to show vulnerability;
- whether they provide information of the same quality and quantity to all students regardless of their learning readiness.

Acknowledging the above issues shows an awareness of unbalanced power relations between teachers and students; but they also show the teachers' conscious actions to address them.

Information is neither neutral nor homogeneous (Babe, 1995). They only appear as such because some have the power to define information for the rest. As members of the public, we should be conscious that better information is not necessarily objective or value free. Better information is by nature embedded in social relations, enabled by technologies, and is heterogeneous and varying. If information is never objective or value-free, then how can we evaluate it?

I propose that the concept "value" is essential for us to evaluate information, what values we treasure in life (such as freedom, democracy, family, friendship, and so on) and how we see the *use value* of information. To explain, when we produce, distribute and use information, we should see it as both the process and end goals of our values. Sometimes our values can be broad and abstract, such as democracy, peace, or economic and social justice. At other times, our values can be deeply personal, such as good health or spirituality. If we allow our values to guide how we produce and use information, we affirm the importance of collective actions because there may be common values shared by the world population.

Instead of pretending information can be objective and value-free, we should re-discover the use value of information. At present, the exchange value of information is privileged over its use value. In Chapter 6, "Creating", I show that digital media have enabled many to produce information for free, but large platform companies exploited the labor and affects of many content producers. The profits of some information companies come from users' free labor. While some proposed that information companies should pay users for their invisible labor, this will only reinforce the capitalistic belief that only exchange value matters. If everything—including our idle time and free labor—can be assigned an exchange value, then we choose to neglect the use value of resources, such as our time and affects. The value that needs to be re-ascribed to information is use value; we need to consider what is useful for us as social beings and as community members. When we acknowledge use value of information, it means that we establish social relations with others when we produce information. To give a simple, non-information example: mothers breastfeed their babies because breast milk has use value. In addition, breastfeeding bonds mothers with babies, teaching babies that they are part of a social relation. Similarly, when we produce information that has use value, we not only ask ourselves how we increase the wealth of the commons, but also how we bind one person to others in community-building.

Recognizing the constitutive relationship between information, technology, and society also addresses the unbalanced power relation that underlines production, distribution, and consumption. If we see information being "outside" society and technology, then information would appear to be a neutral object that exists "out there" with little human interference. Information would appear to be like air and water that is passively waiting for humans to use it. Throughout the book, I argue that information is not *outside* a society, but *constitutes* it. What it means is that the kind of information produced and circulated in a society makes it a particular kind of society. For example, in Chapter 3, "Searching", I argued that humans had established a number of systems to organize information for others to search. All of these systems had created a specific kind of society. For example, dictionaries standardize language usage, making one kind of speech more socially acceptable than others. By categorizing some words as slang, dictionaries created a society where users' linguistic choice defines their social position.

Information is also not external to the technology which produces, distributes, and consumes it (Melody, 1993). In other words, information does not exist independently of technology, it picks up the property of technology through its production, distribution, and consumption (see Chapter 4, "Accessing"). One implication of the interdependent relation between information and technology is that those who control technology have a better chance to control how information is used. For example, search engines do not simply organize information, they use algorithms to create hierarchy of information. Another implication of an acknowledged interdependent relation between information and technology is that information technology will be recognized to be as heterogeneous and varying as information. Even though there are a lot of digital devices to choose from in the market, they all set up a specific way for users to interact with technology. For example, we all expect digital devices to have Internet connectivity regardless of its necessity. To unsettle unequal power relations, users should acknowledge that technological devices do not need to produce the same kind of information. In addition, analogue technologies are not necessarily outdated or antiquated, they can be more effective at challenging unequal power relations in some circumstances. For example, street protestors often opt to use homemade signage with recycled cardboard. Homemade signboards may not look professional or polished, but they convey powerful information by reflecting protestors' values and connecting like-minded people in a community.

QUESTION 3: HOW CAN WE SEE OURSELVES AS CREATORS, CRITICS, AND ACTIVISTS OF INFORMATION?

When we understand that more and faster information is not better and there are multiple ways to define good information, we need to take actions to challenge the power that defines, controls, and creates information. We can only take actions when we begin to see ourselves as creators, critics, and activists of information.

Individuals may feel powerless and helpless after learning about the power of institutions and they may feel they cannot change anything. In addition, for populations who are traditionally given less power to create and control information, they may feel it is impossible to tilt an unbalanced power relation. Some individuals try to resist hegemonic power by giving out false information to sway others' opinions. For example, the conspiracy group QAnon loosely organized themselves online. They believe that they resist societal elites such as politicians, journalists, and entertainers by falsely spreading information about a "deep state" of Satan-worshipping pedophiles ("What is QAnon?", 2020).

Others may resist hegemonic power by choosing a "less evil" company. For example, Apple was once seen as a "good" company that countered IBM; Google was seen as less evil than Microsoft. But Apple Computers and Google have become bigger companies than both IBM and Microsoft. The monopolistic tendencies of these once good companies are no different from the "evil" power that they once challenged.

The aforementioned two ways to counter hegemony—spreading false information and choosing a "less evil" company—rely on false choices: users have to choose between giving out truthful or false information; consumers choose between one product, one brand, or one company over others. In addition, both kinds of actions lock users in a passive consumer position; consumers are only able to act at decisions that have already been made for them. I argue that to be an active participant in information means we need to make decisions for ourselves.

To actively change power relations that are constructed in and through information, we need to first recognize our sense of agency. According to Giddens (1984), individual agency and social structure is mutually constitutive. If we wish to change social structure, we need to exercise our sense of agency. The first step to exercise agency is to shift the position from being users and consumers of packaged information to that of being creators, critics, and activists. How we see ourselves in relation to information matters, especially for populations who traditionally have been seen as recipients of resources.

To create information does not necessarily mean we will need years of schooling to learn statistics and programming because the ability to create is inherent in most humans. To create is to exercise praxis, which is essential to change social structure. When we create, we claim ownership of our own creation and we connect to each other (Leach, 2005). When we create, we think about our audience and how we may bring "good" information to others. To critique is to occupy a particular standpoint to see the world. For example, this book has provided one way to critique information. It asks us to consider unbalanced power relations in the production, distribution, and consumption of information. But this is only one standpoint. Some prefers other standpoints, such as critiquing information from a regulation or legal view, or becoming activists on the local or global stage, or working for non-profit organizations.

As creators, critics, and activists, we need to understand the social positions of others, which mean taking an interest in others who have different social positions from us. Social positions are formed by race, ethnicity, gender, sexual orientation, social class, and other factors; they are also formed by family configurations and responsibilities; native and primary languages; professions and hobbies; religious and spiritual beliefs. In the subway passenger example given in the Introduction, I ask that we put ourselves in the shoes of another person so that we can understand why and how someone, who is not like us, interacts with information in a specific way. If we are able to do so, when the subway train finally reaches its destination, we will emerge from it and see the world differently.

BIBLIOGRAPHY

Anthias, F. (2012). Hierarchies of social location, class and intersectionality: Towards a translocational frame. *International Sociology, 28*(1), 121–138.

Babe, R. E. (1995). *Communication and the transformation of economics: Essays in information, public policy, and political economy.* Boulder, CO: Westview Press.

Babe, R. E. (2011). The place of information in economics. In E. A. Comor (Ed.), *Media, structures, and power: The Robert E. Babe collection* (pp. 22–42). Toronto: University of Toronto Press.

Cooks, L., & Isgro, K. (2005). The "cyber Summit" and women: Incorporating gender into information and communication technology UN policies. *Frontiers: A Journal of Women's Studies, 26*(1), 71–89.

Crawford, R. (1996). Computer-assisted crises. In G. Gerbner, H. Mowlana, & H. I. Schiller (Eds.), *Invisible crises: What conglomerate control of media means for America and the world* (pp. 47–81). Boulder, CO: Westview Press.

Giddens, A. (1984). *The constitution of society: Outline of the theory of structuration.* Berkeley, CA: University of California Press.

Harvey, D. (1989). *The condition of postmodernity: An enquiry into the origins of cultural change.* Cambridge, MA: Blackwell.

Hassan, R. (2008). *The information society.* Cambridge, UK: Polity.

Henwood, F., Wyatt, S., Miller, N., & Senker, P. (2000). Critical perspectives on technologies, in/equalities and the information society. In S. Wyatt, F. Henwood, N. Miller, & P. Senker (Eds.), *Technology and in/equality: Questioning the information society* (pp. 1–18). New York: Routledge.

Leach, J. (2005). Modes of creativity and the register of ownership. In R. A. Ghosh (Ed.), *Code: Collaborative ownership and the digital economy* (pp. 30–44). Cambridge, MA: MIT Press.

Melody, W. H. (1993). In J. Wasko, V. Mosco, & M. Pendakur (Eds.) *Illuminating the blindspot: Essays honoring Dallas W. Smythe* (pp. 63–81). Norwood, NJ: Ablex.

Munyua, H. (2000). Application of ICTs in Africa's agricultural sector: A gender perspective. In E. M. Rathgeber & E. O. Adera (Eds.) *Gender and the information revolution in Africa* (pp. 85–123). Ottawa, Canada: International Development Research Centre.

Postone, M. (1993). *Time, labor, and social domination: A reinterpretation of Marx's critical theory.* Cambridge, UK: Cambridge University Press.

Radloff, J., & Primo, N. (2002). Net gains for women in Africa. *Development, 45*(4), 41–48.

Totty, M. (2020, November 4). How to make AI less biased. *Wall Street Journal,* p. R1.

Webster, F. (2006). *Theories of information society* (3rd ed.). Abingdon, UK: Routledge.

"What is Qanon?" (2020, October 15). *Wall Street Journal.* Retrieved from: https://www.wsj.com/articles/what-is-qanon-what-we-know-about-the-conspiracy-theory-11597694801

INDEX

activists 20, 124, 145–6, 161–3
advertising 63, 129, 154, 156
African Americans 50, 96; in U.S. census 116–22, 176 *see also* United States census
agency: of machines 13, 20; social actors' exercise of 12, 29, 172–4, 184
algorithm *see* computer codes
Alphabet (company) 17–18, 158, 160
Amazon (company) 42, 131–6
American Library Association (ALA) 73–5
analogue 2, 27, 53, 67, 72, 83, 143, 182
artists 145, 161–3
Association for Information Science and Technology (ASIS&T) 33
Association of American Colleges and Universities (AAC&U) 73
Association of College and Research Libraries (ACRL) 75–6

Bell, Daniel 40–4, 47
bias: class 29; gender 29, 49, 52, 113, 123; racial 29, 39, 49, 52, 113, 115, 120, 176; western 59, 67, 69–70, 74–5
Big Data 114, 130–3, 135
biology: molecular 37–8, 46, 50
Blacks *see* African Americans
British Empire 70

Castells, Manuel 29, 42–4
China: identity card 115, 124; protests against 129; telecommunications 17
citizenship: digital 91, 94, 97–102; relationship to information 21–2, 75, 107–8

class: exploitation between 9, 150, 154, 161, 166; identities 10; oppression 8; relations 9; ruling 9–10; working 136, 159
codes: computer 133, 151, 156, 163, 176, 182; genetic *see also* biology; open source 163–5; protected 114, 132, 155, 158, 163
Cold War 127, 152
Committee on Public Information 31
Common Sense Media 98–9
census 112–13, 114–122, 136–7, 176
colonialism 70
concept: abstract 27–8; neutral 28–30, 45, 52; physical 38–9
consumption: of information 4, 16, 81, 143, 152, 172, 182, 184; habits 5, 112, 154
copyleft *see* intellectual property
corporations 10–13, 93–4, 99, 106, 108, 111–12, 130–6, 174
COVID-19 7, 11, 15, 98, 134
Creative Commons 164
critical cultural studies 10, 16, 21
critical race theories 13–16, 21
Cutter, Charles Ammi 60
cybersecurity 32, 112–13

databases: online 34, 53, 74
democracy 36, 73, 94–5, 127, 129, 137, 181
Dewey, John 94–7, 102, 107
dictionary 58–9, 62–3, 71
directory: online 66–7, telephone 58, 64–5
disinformation 114, 125, 127–30
DNA 36–7, 46–7, 53

economy: affect 12; information 30, 39–40, 42–52; platform 11
encyclopedia 58, 61–2
entropy 38
eurocentrism 70
experience: embodied 68

Facebook 129, 153, 176
Frankfurt School 8–9
Federal Communications Commission (FCC) 103
feminism: post-feminism 14–15; theories 13–14

gender: inequality of 7, 19, 116; relations 14, 16, 29, 48–9; *see also* bias
genome mapping 37, 39, 47, 49–50, 121
goods: common 8, 151; cultural 5; inexhaustivity of 22, 147, 150–1, 157, 161, 164–5; private 8, 99; public 104, 113, 136, 145; social 4, 113; tangible 41, 144–5, 147–8
governance 89–90
governments 91, 93–4, 104–5, 112–14; agency 102–3; role in record-keeping 115, 123–4, 137 *see also* United States census
governmentality 101
Greenwich Mean Time (GMT) 63–4, 70
Gulf War 111, 125, 137

Hall, Stuart 10, 86, 88
homelessness 97–102, 105, 107, 121
Hong Kong 129

identity cards: national 113, 115, 122–124, 137, 177
ideology 9–10
illiteracy *see* literacy
immigrants 7, 51, 95–6, 107, 118, 120–4, 136,
information and communication technologies (ICT) 11, 90–1, 143, 165
intellectual property 41, 93, 145, 151–2, 156–66 *see also* World Intellectual Property Organization (WIPO); copyleft 146, 163, 166, 174
International Telecommunication Union (ITU) 91–4
Inuit 68–9
Islamophobia 114, 126, 137

knowledge: commons 146; cultural 42, 89; disembedded 49, 68–9, 74–6; homogenization of 70–2

Latinx 97, 119–20
library 174; catalogue 60; library sciences 34–6, 46–8; as a space 99–102
Library of Congress 69, 142–3
Lippmann, Walter 94–7, 102, 107
literacy: definition of information literacy 59, 72–7, 111; illiteracy 173; mass literacy 21, 174; rate of 143
Liverpool and Manchester Railway 63

Marx, Karl 9, 146, 148–9
mathematics model of communication 35, 37–9
map 2, 45–6, 65–6, 68, 70, 72
mathematics 35, 37–9
McLuhan, Marshall 84–6, 92, 106
media: broadcast 87, 103–4, 107; hot/cold 88, 106; mass 9–10, 35, 94–5, 97, 107
misinformation *see* disinformation
Moore, Gordon 175

Netflix 130, 133–5
networks: images of 29; as in Science and Technology Studies 17–18; network society 42–4, 51
newspapers 63, 88–9, 179
North African population 112, 121

Obama, Barack 80–3, 102, 104, 128
Ong, Walter 86–9
Oracle 130–1
oral culture 87–8, 106

orality *see* oral culture
Organisation for Economic Co-operation and Development (OECD) 43–4, 47

participation: audience 85–6, political 21
political economy 10–11, 13, 144–6, 156, 160–1
power: hegemonic 183; inequality of 7, 19, 39, 80; political 123; relations 92–4, 174, 179-80, 183; social 6; symbolic 16; working of 16–7, 77, 88–90, 130, 132, 172, 184
Prime Meridian 64, 70
printing 68, 87–8
privatization: of information 11, 145–6, 161–5; of space 102
public interest 82, 89, 94, 102–5, 107–8, 162–3
public opinion 31, 127, 129
public utilities 104–5

race: harassment of 15, 126; segregation of 15; *see also* bias
railway: British Railway 63, 71; U.S. 65
Rand McNally 65–6
racism 15, 82, 127
Russia 127–9, 137, 176

science: applied 35; human 34; library 30, 32–4, 38, 46–7, 50; natural 34–5; social 34–5
Shannon, Claude 35, 37–9, 84–5, 88, 92, 106
slave questionnaire 116–17
smartphones 13, 15, 153
space: private 102, 107; public 99–101, 107
social capital 12, 105

social justice 10, 128
social relations 7, 9, 16, 39, 179–81
society: closed 5; network 42–4; open 5; post-industrial 40–1, 47
standardization of time 3, 63–5, 71
statistics 28, 32, 34

telecommunications 10, 17, 103
time: labor 9, 148–51, 156, 160–1, 164; local 63, 71; travel 71
transmission model of communication *see* mathematics model of communication
Trump, Donald 96, 121, 126–9
Twitter 20, 129

United Kingdom 123–4
United Nations Educational, Scientific and Cultural Organization (UNESCO) 90–3
United States: census 112, 115–22, 136–7, 176; intellectuals in 94–5, 107
USA Patriot Act 126

value: exchange 146–50, 159–61, 163–5, 181; social 4; use 146–51, 159, 161, 163, 165, 181–2

War on Terror 114, 125–5, 137
Weaver, Warren 35, 37–9, 84–5, 88, 92
work: paid 4, 14, 144, 150; unpaid 12, 14, 144
World Intellectual Property Organization (WIPO) 157
writing 87–8
WWII 17, 33, 90

Yahoo! 66